Big Book of Dot-to-Dots and More!

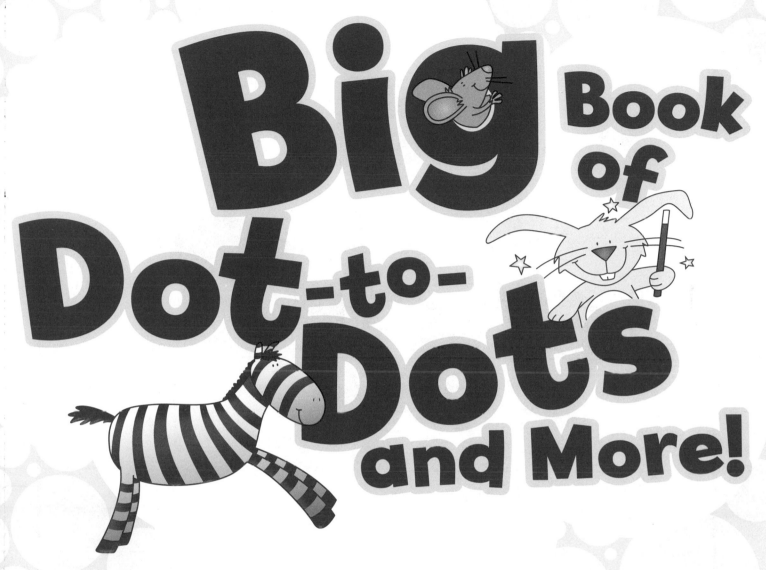

Illustrations by
Small World Design

© 2008, Rainbow Bridge Publishing, Greensboro, North Carolina 27425. The purchase of this material entitles the buyer to reproduce worksheets and activities for classroom use only—not for commercial resale. Reproduction of these materials for an entire school or district is prohibited. No part of this book may be reproduced (except as noted above), stored in a retrieval system, or transmitted in any form or by any means (mechanically, electronically, recording, etc.) without the prior written consent of Rainbow Bridge Publishing.

Printed in the USA • All rights reserved.

ISBN 978-1-60095-372-9

Connect the dots from **a** to **f**. Start at the ★.
Color the picture.

© Rainbow Bridge Publishing

Connect the dots from **A** to **F**. Start at the ★.
Color the picture.

Connect the dots from **a** to **k**. Start at the ★.
Color the picture.

© Rainbow Bridge Publishing

Color each space to find the hidden picture.

△ = pink   ○ = yellow

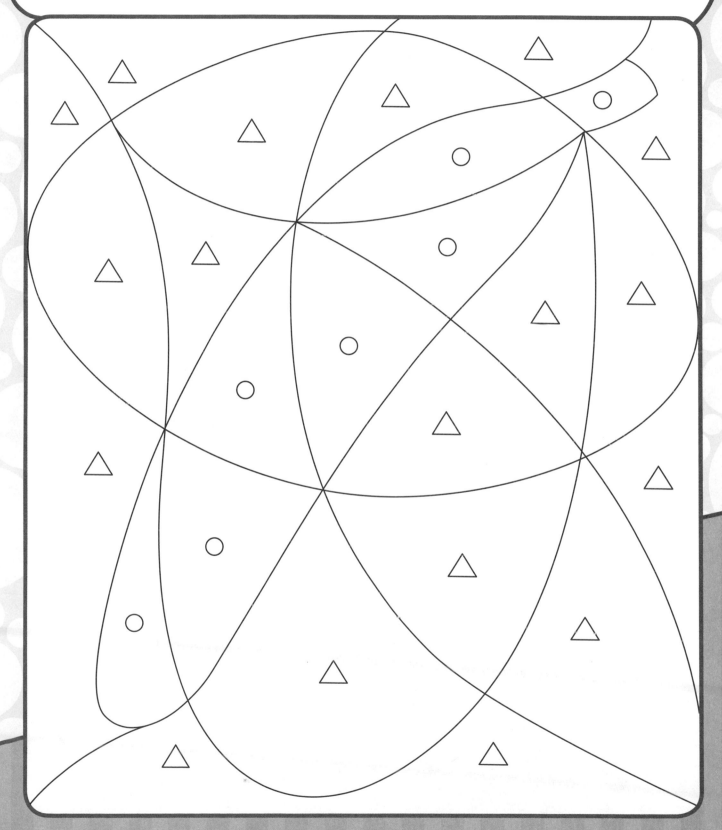

Connect the dots from **1** to **5**. Start at the ★. Color the picture.

© Rainbow Bridge Publishing

Connect the dots from **a** to **f**. Start at the ★.
Color the picture.

Connect the dots from **a** to **k**. Start at the ★.
Color the picture.

© Rainbow Bridge Publishing

Cut out each object. Paste the objects on the picture.

cut ✂

© Rainbow Bridge Publishing

Connect the dots from **1** to **5**. Start at the ★.
Color the picture.

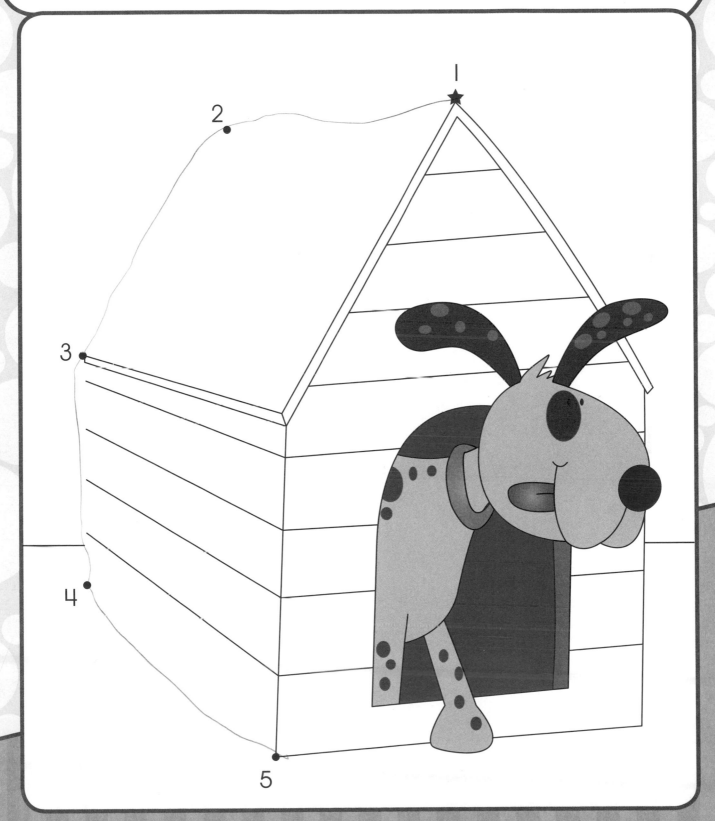

© Rainbow Bridge Publishing

Color each space to find the hidden picture.

◯ = blue △ = yellow

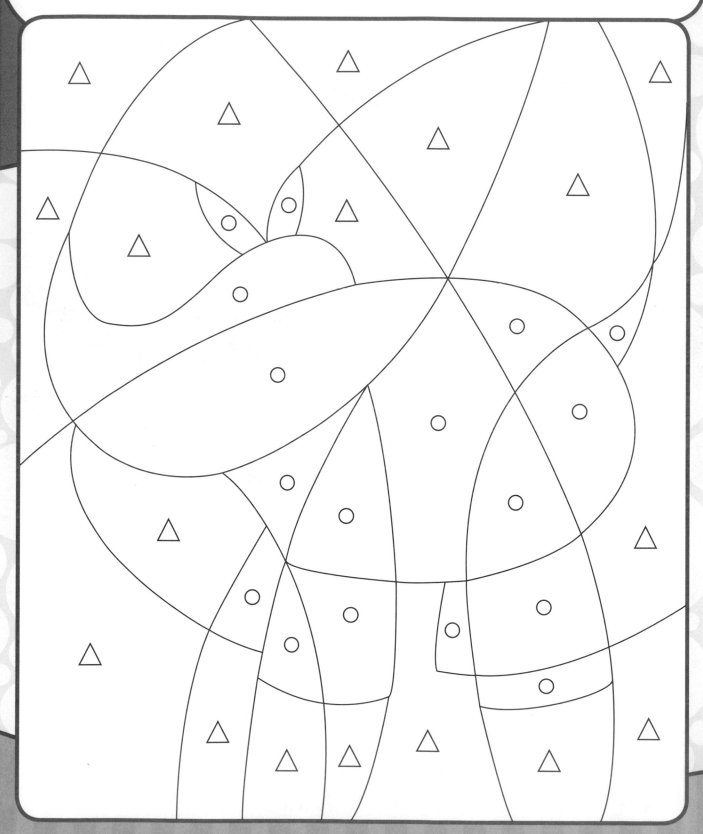

© Rainbow Bridge Publishing

Connect the dots from **A** to **K**. Start at the ★.
Color the picture.

Connect the dots from **I** to **5**. Start at the ★.
Color the picture.

© Rainbow Bridge Publishing

Cut out the puzzle pieces. Put the puzzle together.

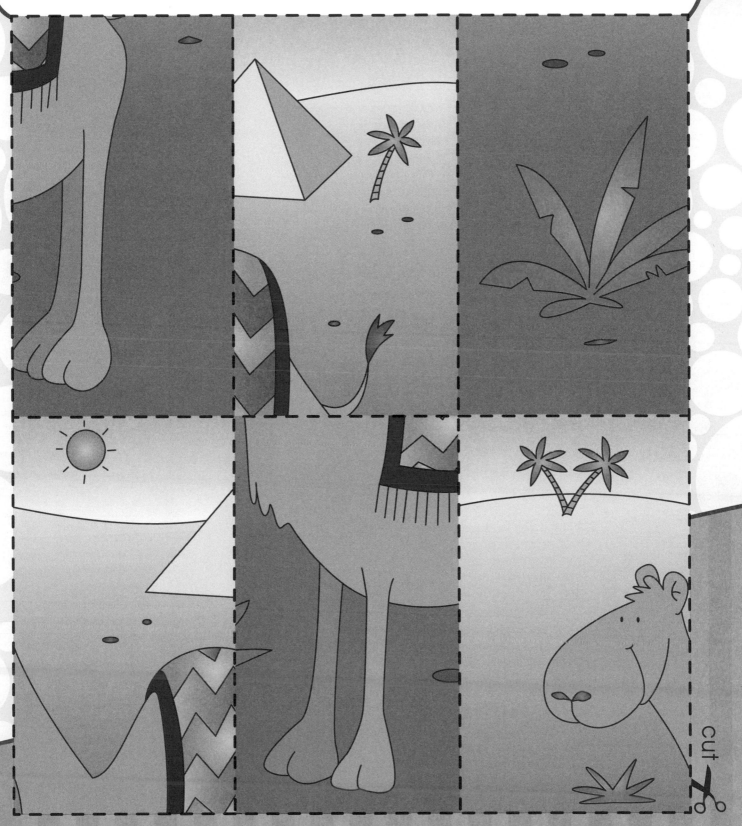

cut

Connect the dots from **A** to **K**. Start at the ★.
Color the picture.

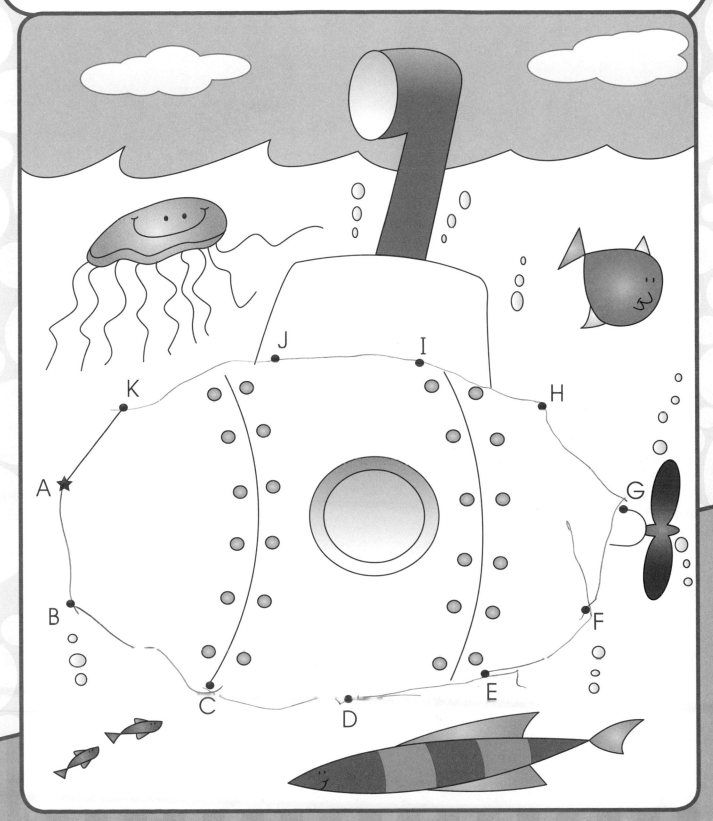

Draw a line to help the bees
find the center of the flower.

© Rainbow Bridge Publishing

Connect the dots from **1** to **10**. Start at the ★.
Color the picture.

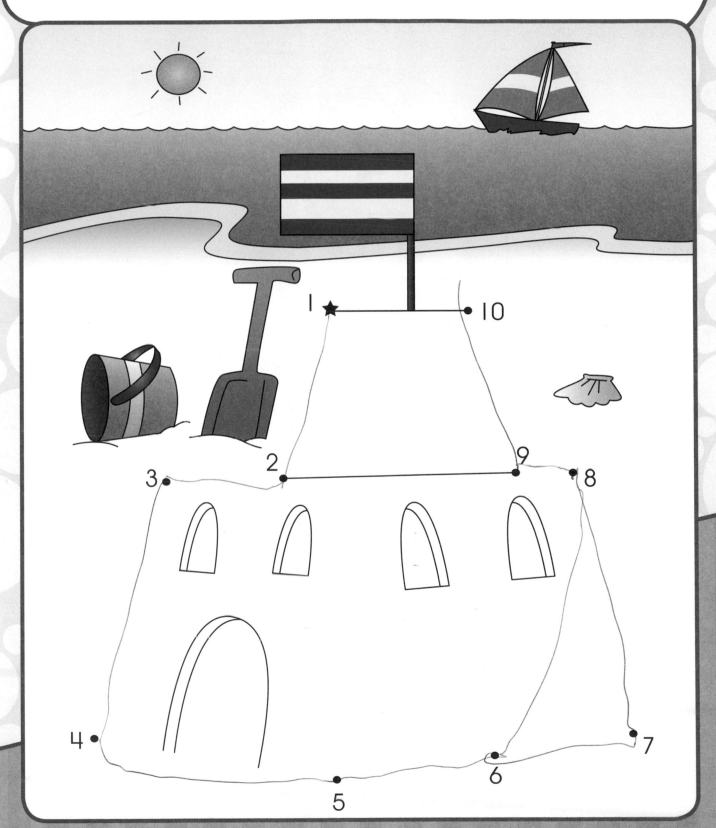

Connect the dots from **a** to **k**. Start at the ★.
Color the picture.

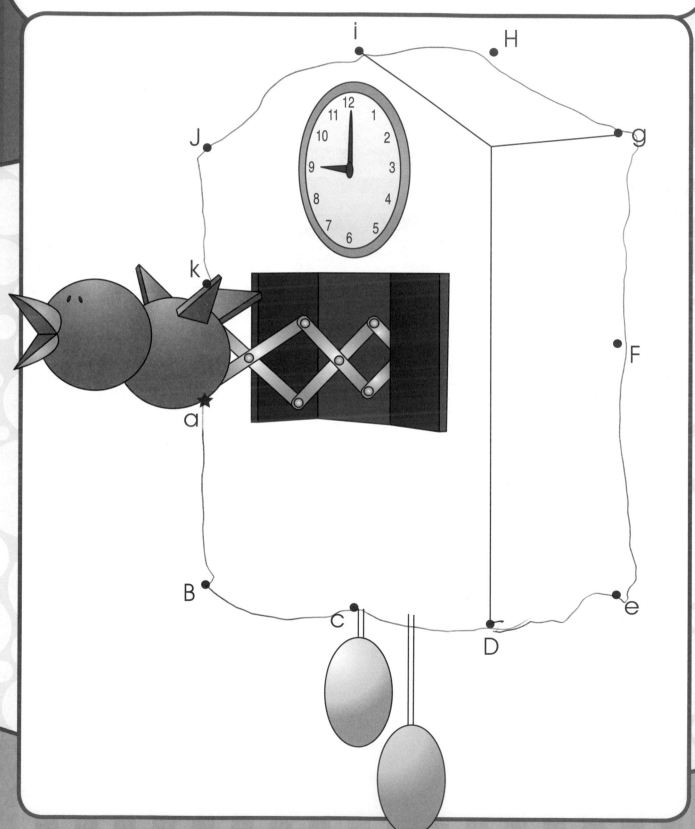

© Rainbow Bridge Publishing

Cut out each object. Paste the objects on the picture.

cut

Connect the dots from **1** to **10**. Start at the ★.
Color the picture.

Use a different color crayon to trace each line.
Which hat is the girl wearing?

© Rainbow Bridge Publishing

Connect the dots from **1** to **10**. Start at the ★.
Color the picture.

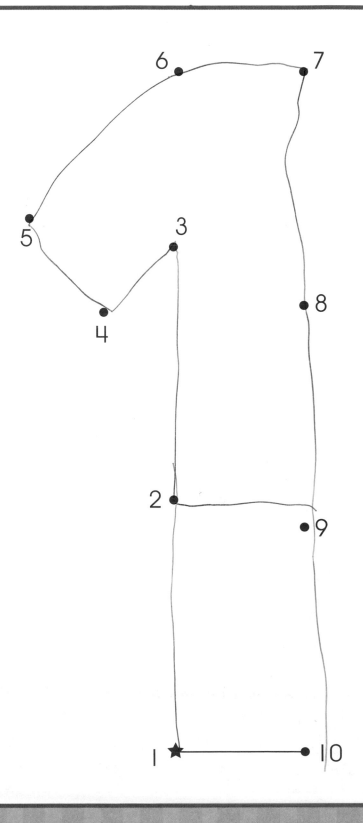

Connect the dots from **A** to **K**. Start at the ★.
Color the picture.

© Rainbow Bridge Publishing

Cut out each object. Paste the objects on the picture.

cut

Connect the dots from **1** to **10**. Start at the ★.
Color the picture.

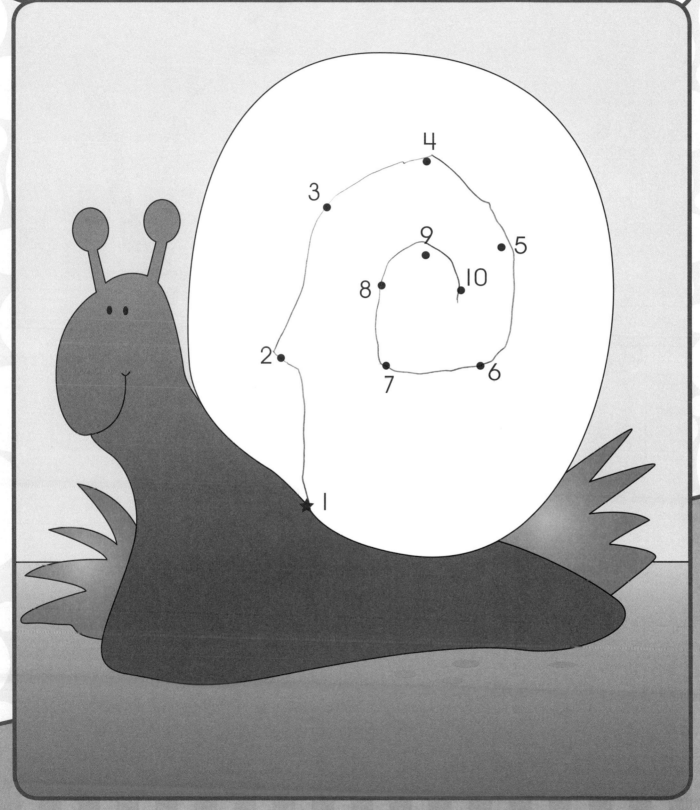

Connect the dots from **a** to **k**. Start at the ★.
Color the picture.

a

b

c

d

e   f   g   h

i

j

k

© Rainbow Bridge Publishing

Color each space to find the hidden picture.

Y = yellow   P = purple

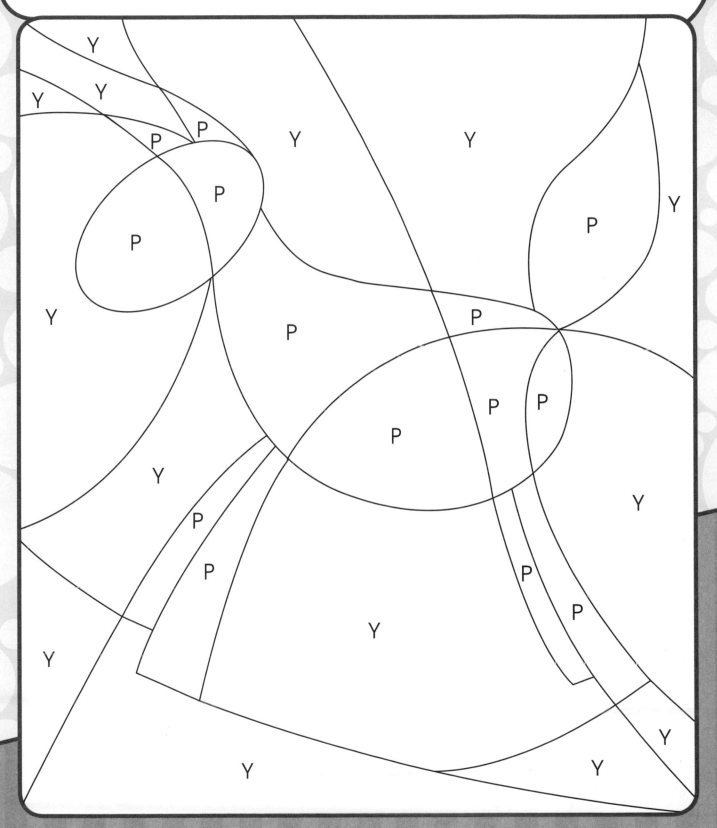

© Rainbow Bridge Publishing

Connect the dots from **1** to **10**. Start at the ★.
Color the picture.

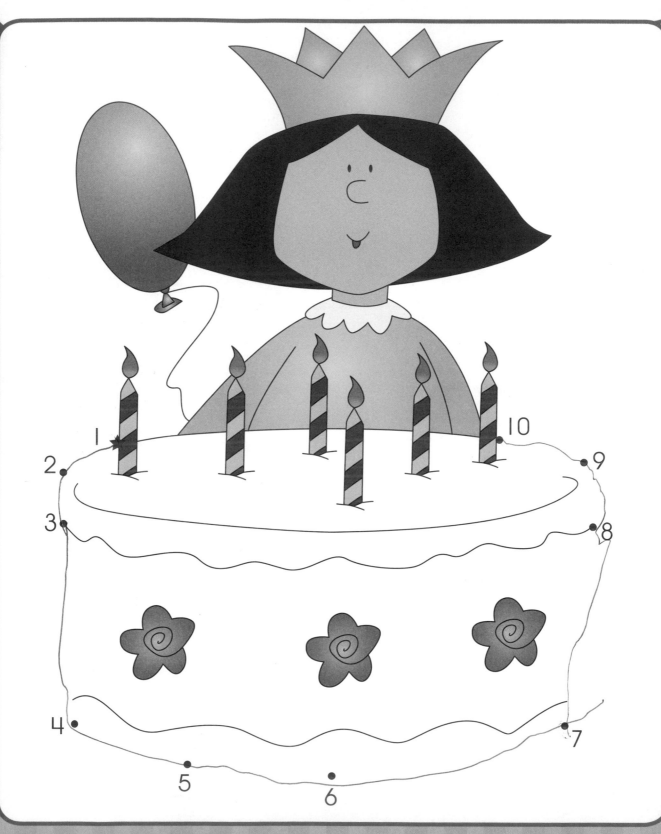

© Rainbow Bridge Publishing

Cut out the puzzle pieces. Put the puzzle together.

cut

Connect the dots from **a** to **k**. Start at the ★.
Color the picture.

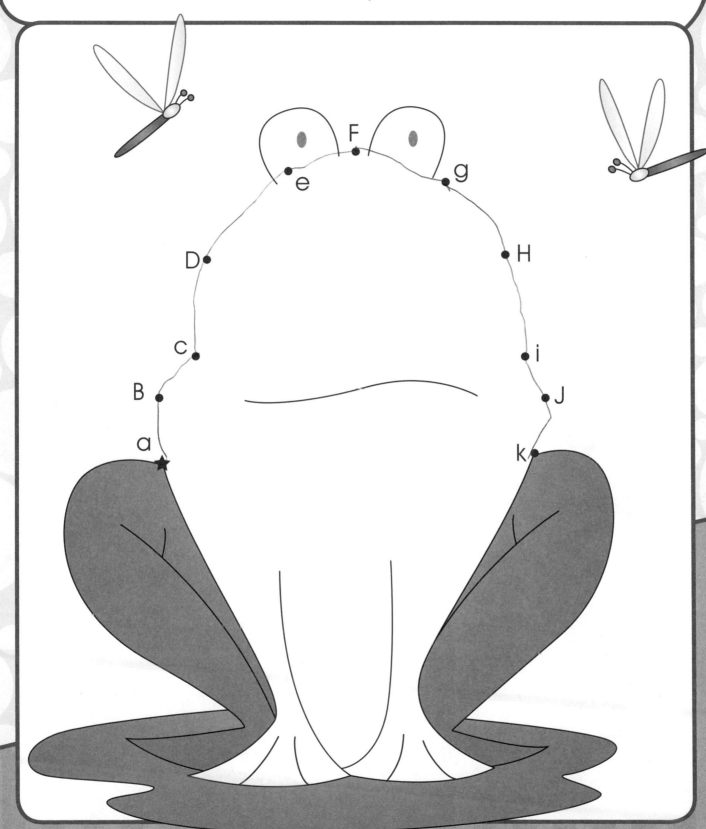

Connect the dots from **I** to **I0**. Start at the ★.
Color the picture.

© Rainbow Bridge Publishing

Break the code and find the letters to name a type of insect.

5	E	F	P	E	C
4	N	O	K	T	J
3	Q	B	S	G	R
2	H	L	O	V	D
1	T	I	M	A	H
	A	B	C	D	E

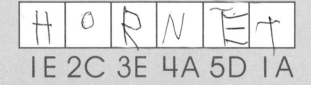

H O R N E T

1E 2C 3E 4A 5D 1A

© Rainbow Bridge Publishing

Connect the dots from **A** to **K**. Start at the ★.
Color the picture.

© Rainbow Bridge Publishing

Cut out each object. Paste the objects on the picture.

cut

Color each space to find the hidden picture.

1 = yellow   2 = red   3 = green

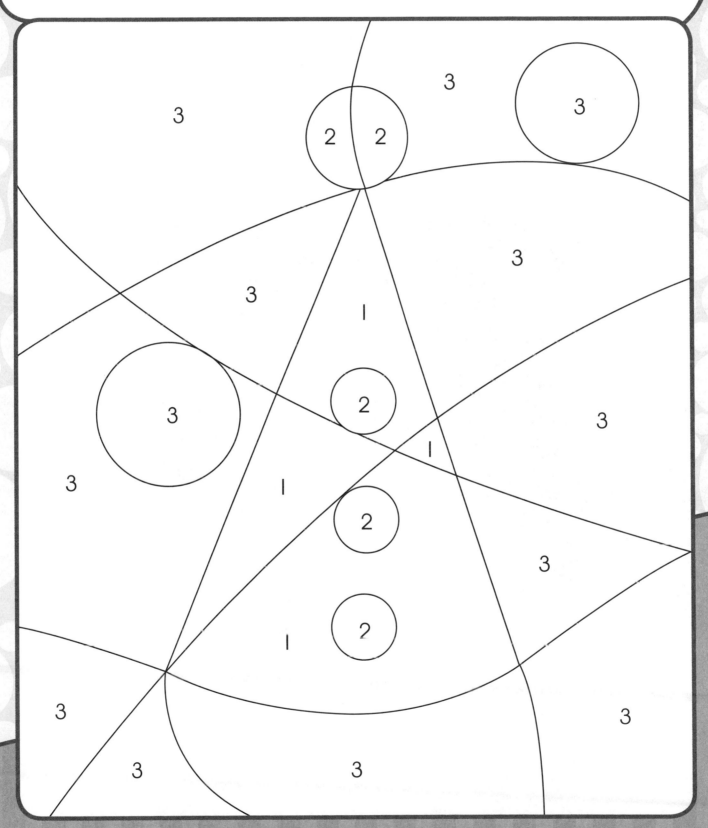

© Rainbow Bridge Publishing

Connect the dots from **I** to **I0**. Start at the ★. Color the picture.

© Rainbow Bridge Publishing

Connect the dots from **a** to **k**. Start at the ★.
Color the picture.

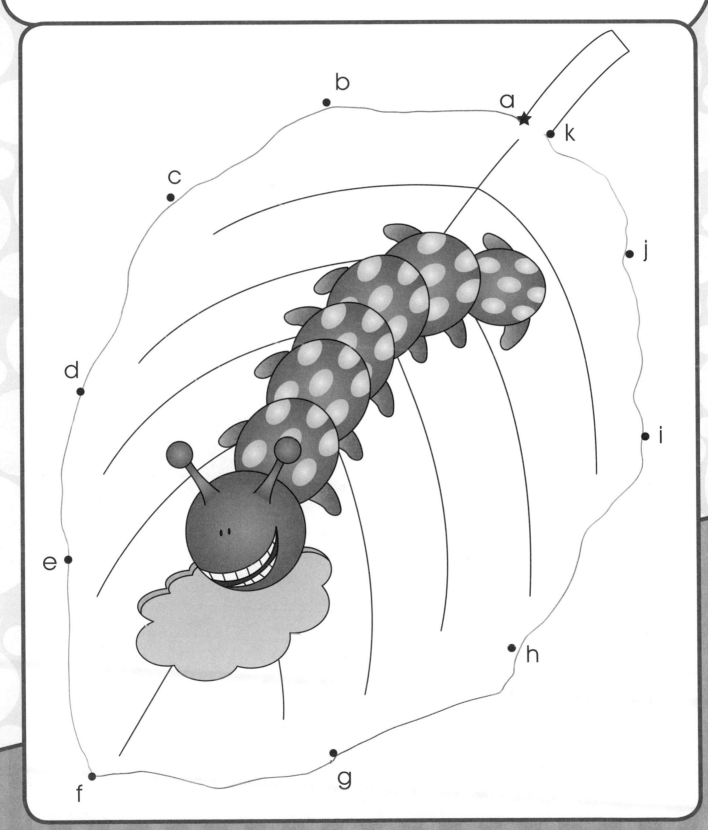

Break the code and find the letters to name a type of dog.

5	R	J	H	T	D
4	S	E	U	L	O
3	N	I	Q	C	X
2	G	V	O	W	F
1	B	M	K	P	A
	A	B	C	D	E

1A	2C	3E	4B	5A

44

© Rainbow Bridge Publishing

Cut out each object. Paste the objects on the picture.

cut

© Rainbow Bridge Publishing

Connect the dots from **1** to **10**. Start at the ★.
Color the picture.

© Rainbow Bridge Publishing

Connect the dots from **A** to **K**. Start at the ★.
Color the picture.

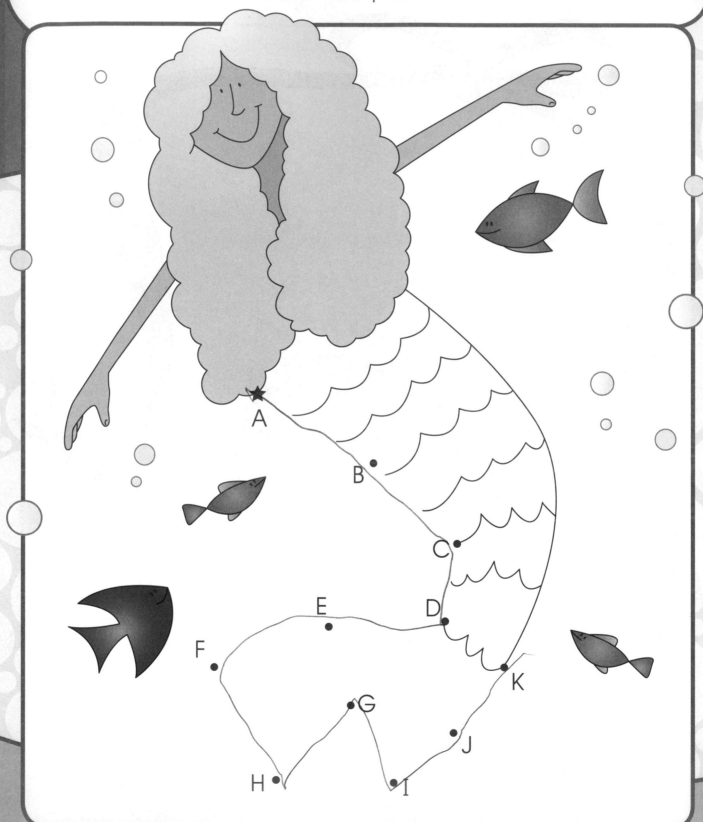

© Rainbow Bridge Publishing

Use a different color crayon to trace each string.
Who is playing with the yo-yo?

© Rainbow Bridge Publishing

Connect the dots from **1** to **10**. Start at the ★. Color the picture.

© Rainbow Bridge Publishing

Cut out the puzzle pieces. Put the puzzle together.

cut

Connect the dots from **a** to **k**. Start at the ★.
Color the picture.

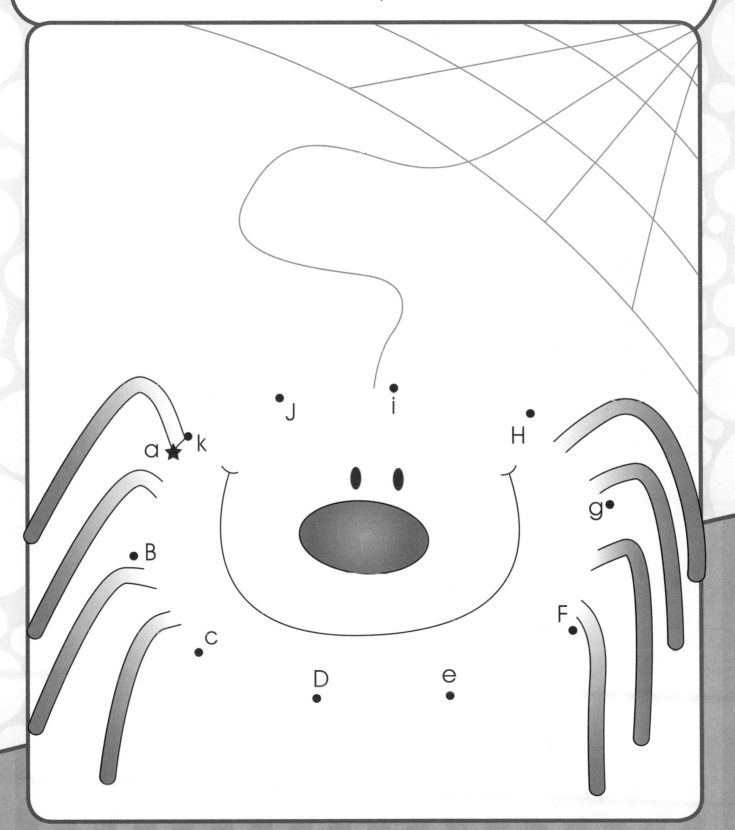

Connect the dots from **1** to **10**. Start at the ★.
Color the picture.

10

1 ★

9

2

8

3

7

6

4

5

© Rainbow Bridge Publishing

Break the code and find the letters to name a type of flower.

5	I	R	H	Q	F
4	P	G	W	A	O
3	D	Z	K	S	J
2	T	L	U	S	B
1	E	Y	C	N	M
	A	B	C	D	E

3A 4D 5A 2D 1B

© Rainbow Bridge Publishing

Connect the dots from **a** to **k**. Start at the ★.
Color the picture.

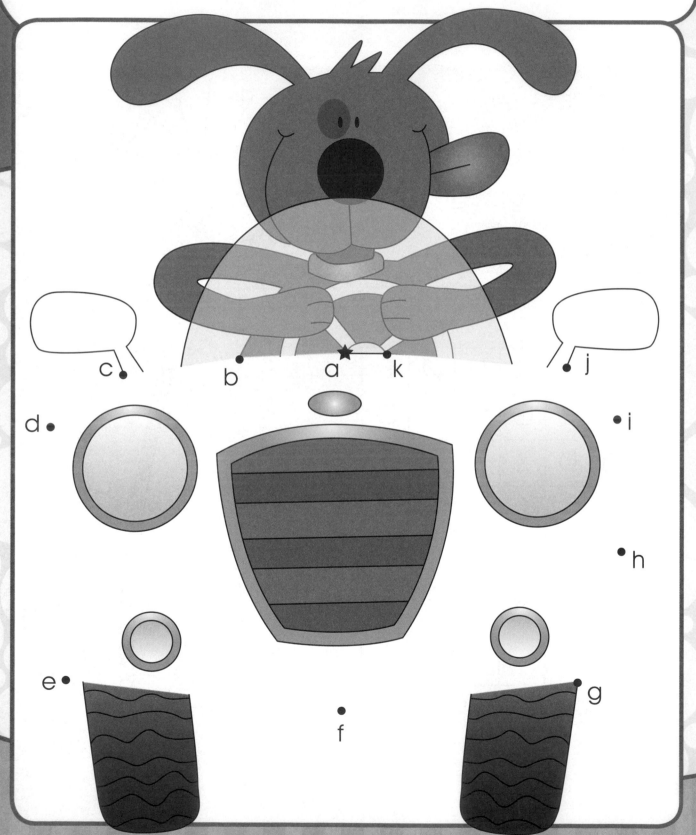

© Rainbow Bridge Publishing

Cut out each fruit. Paste the fruit on the picture.

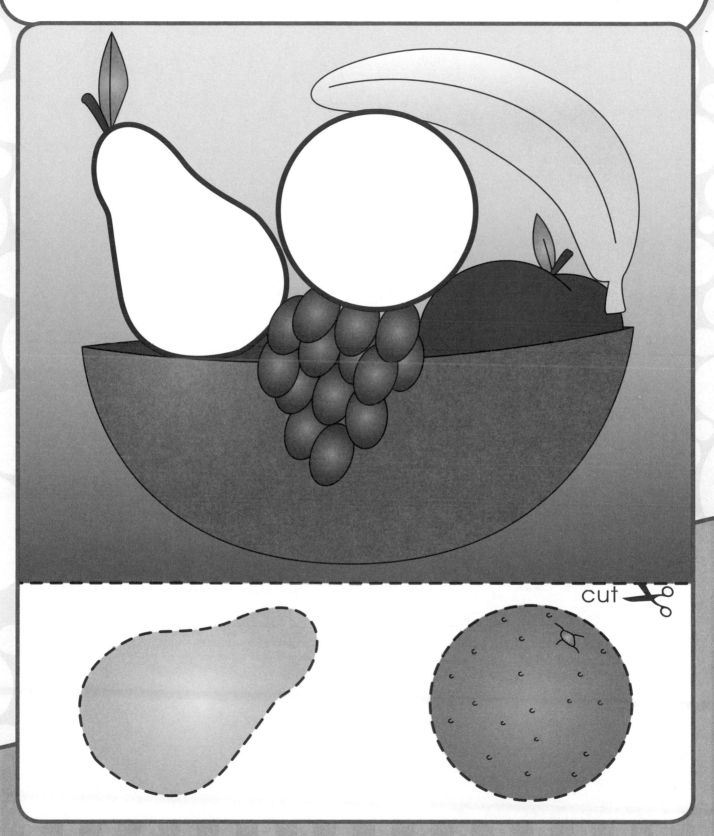

cut

Connect the dots from **1** to **10**. Start at the ★.
Color the picture.

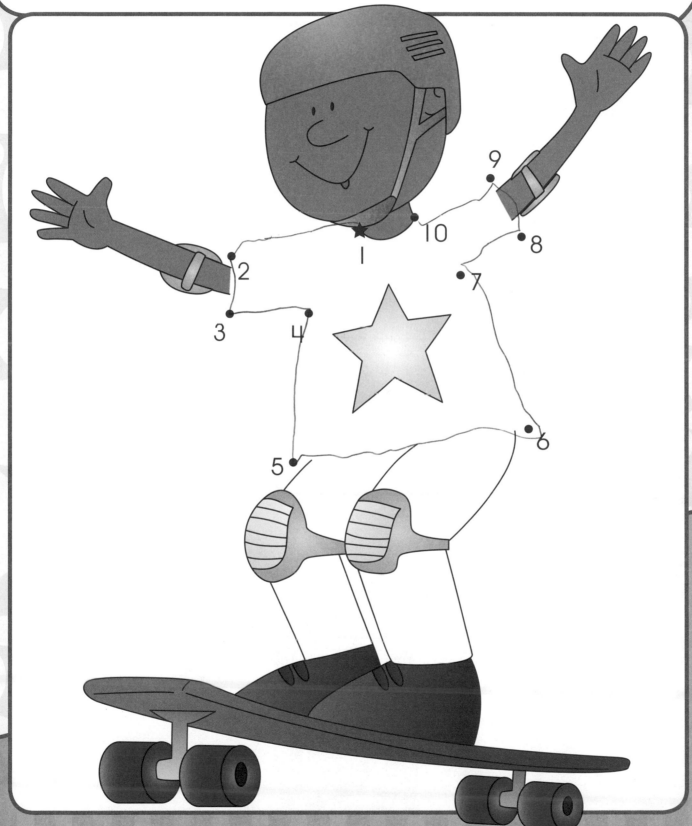

Circle the words hidden in the puzzle.

Word Bank

~~daisy~~ ~~rose~~ ~~lily~~ lilac

l q l m a n l c
s o t d t b y l
w x c y a p e y
u o l r a i d s
l c i s o q s c
i x l w b s m y
l l s a f p s e c
y e c l j w v u

© Rainbow Bridge Publishing

Connect the dots from **1** to **15**. Start at the ★.
Color the picture.

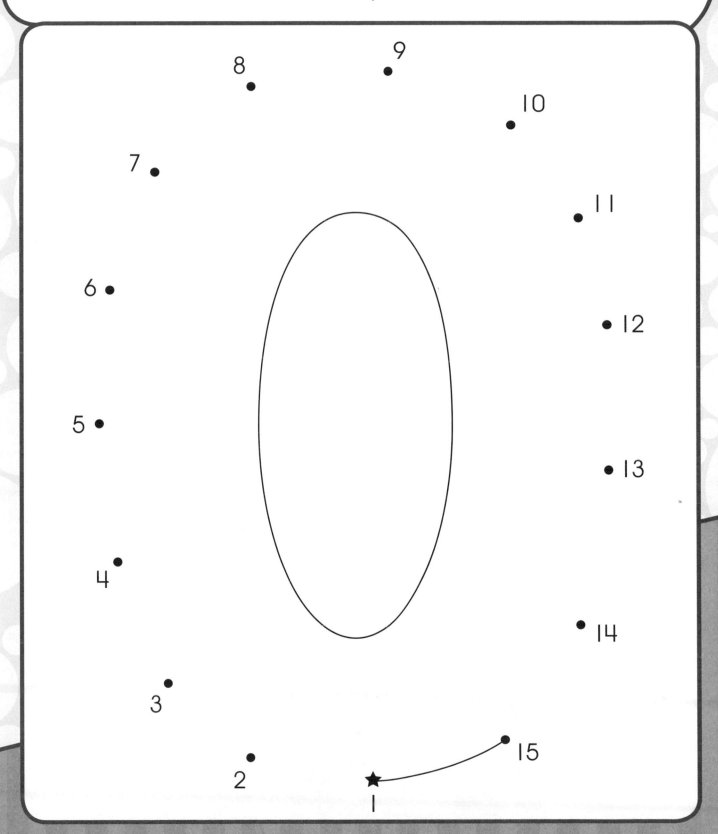

Connect the dots from **A** to **K**. Start at the ★.
Color the picture.

© Rainbow Bridge Publishing

Cut out each object. Paste the objects on the picture.

cut

© Rainbow Bridge Publishing

Connect the dots from **1** to **15**. Start at the ★.
Color the picture.

11

12

13

10

14

9

15

★ 1

8

2

4

7

3

6

5

Circle the words hidden in the picture.

Word Bank

~~hair~~   ~~nose~~   ~~eyes~~   ~~ears~~   ~~lips~~

u	p	x	f	e	k	h	u
c	w	l	b	i	y	k	l
z	h	z	x	w	q	e	a
e	a	l	i	p	s	s	s
y	i	j	b	o	w	r	z
d	r	p	n	j	a	f	z
h	j	a	v	e	m	u	c
n	v	c	j	d	i	e	e

© Rainbow Bridge Publishing

Connect the dots from **a** to **k**. Start at the ★.
Color the picture.

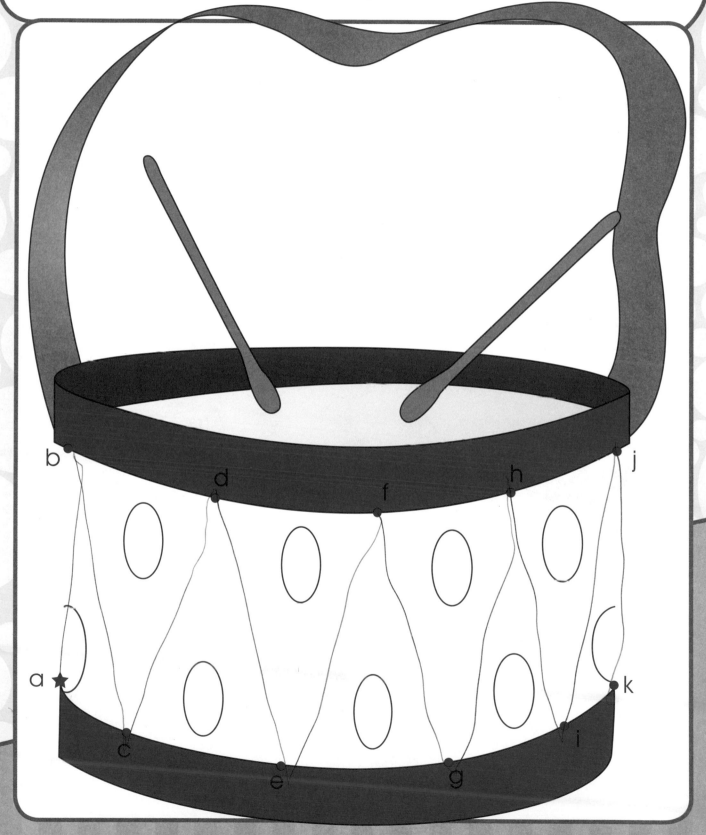

Connect the dots from **1** to **15**. Start at the ★. Color the picture.

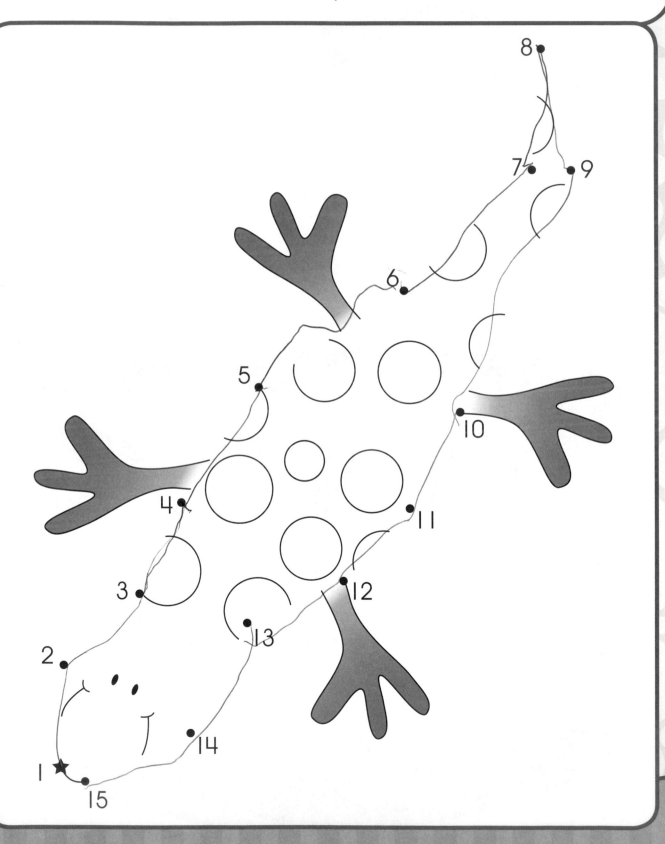

© Rainbow Bridge Publishing

Cut out each object. Paste the objects on the picture.

cut

Circle the words hidden in the puzzle.

Word Bank

mother	father	brother	grandpa
sister	aunt	uncle	grandma

Connect the dots from **A** to **K**. Start at the ★.
Color the picture.

I

J

K

G

E

H

D

C

F

A

B

© Rainbow Bridge Publishing

Connect the dots from **1** to **15**. Start at the ★.
Color the picture.

Connect the dots from **1** to **15**. Start at the ★.
Color the picture.

© Rainbow Bridge Publishing

Cut out the puzzle pieces. Put the puzzle together.

cut

Connect the dots from **a** to **k**. Start at the ★.
Color the picture.

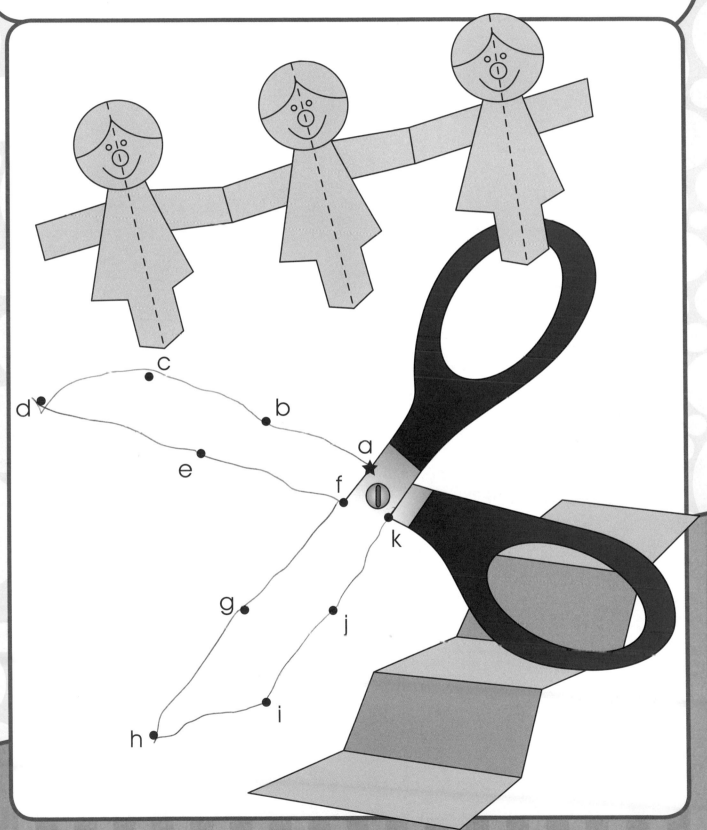

Color each space to find the hidden picture.

☐ = green　　　◇ = pink　　　○ = yellow

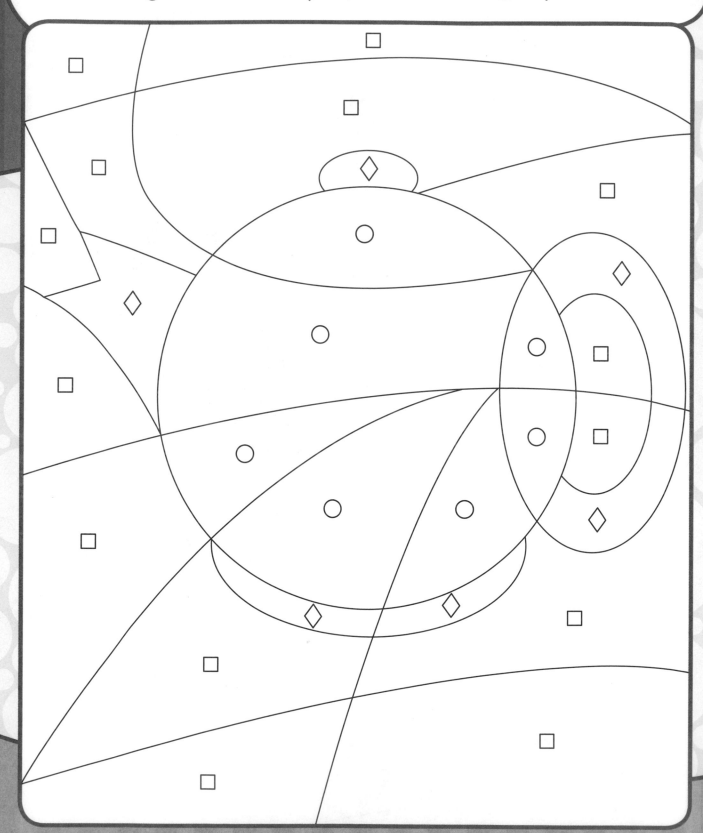

© Rainbow Bridge Publishing

Connect the dots from **a** to **k**. Start at the ★.
Color the picture.

Connect the dots from **A** to **K**. Start at the ★.
Color the picture.

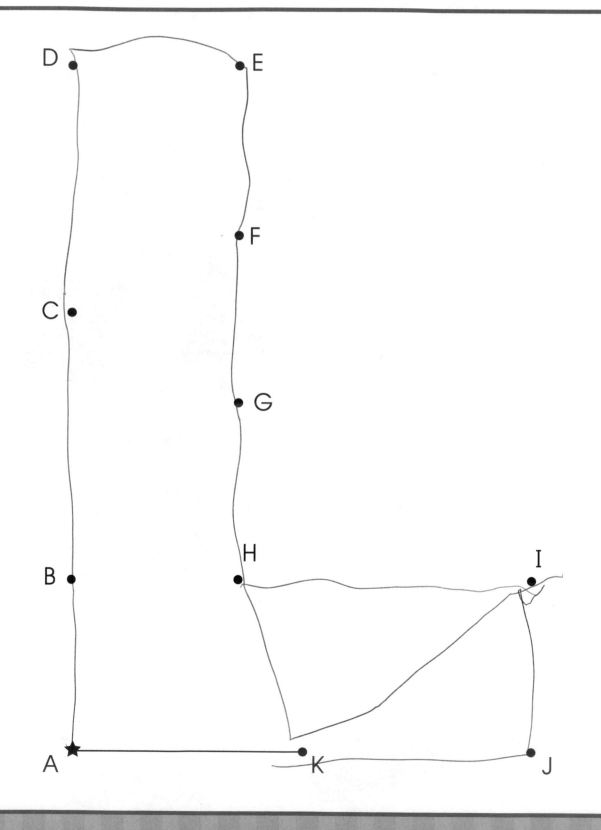

© Rainbow Bridge Publishing

Cut out each object. Paste the objects on the picture.

cut

© Rainbow Bridge Publishing

Connect the dots from **1** to **15**. Start at the ★.
Color the picture.

Circle the words hidden in the puzzle.

Word Bank

hat	skirt	pants	shirt	socks

```
m  w  y  s  c  t  s  u
y  q  h  k  h  s  f  w
x  t  e  i  k  i  u  r
k  c  n  c  p  w  r  m
m  i  o  n  a  m  n  t
l  s  n  b  n  v  a  m
s  k  i  r  t  h  a  v
d  l  y  a  s  x  r  w
```

© Rainbow Bridge Publishing

Connect the dots from **A** to **K**. Start at the ★.
Color the picture.

★ A
K
B
J
I
C
D
H
E
F
G

Connect the dots from **A** to **K**. Start at the ★.
Color the picture.

E •

F •

• G

• D

C •

I •

• H

B •

• J

A ★——————————• K

© Rainbow Bridge Publishing

Cut out each object. Paste the objects on the picture.

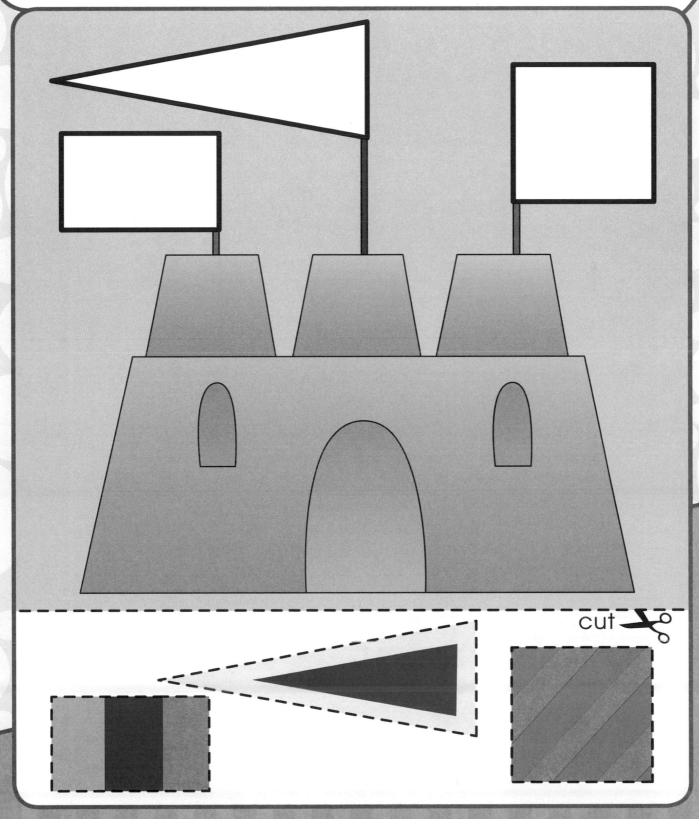

cut ✂

© Rainbow Bridge Publishing

Connect the dots from **A** to **K**. Start at the ★.
Color the picture.

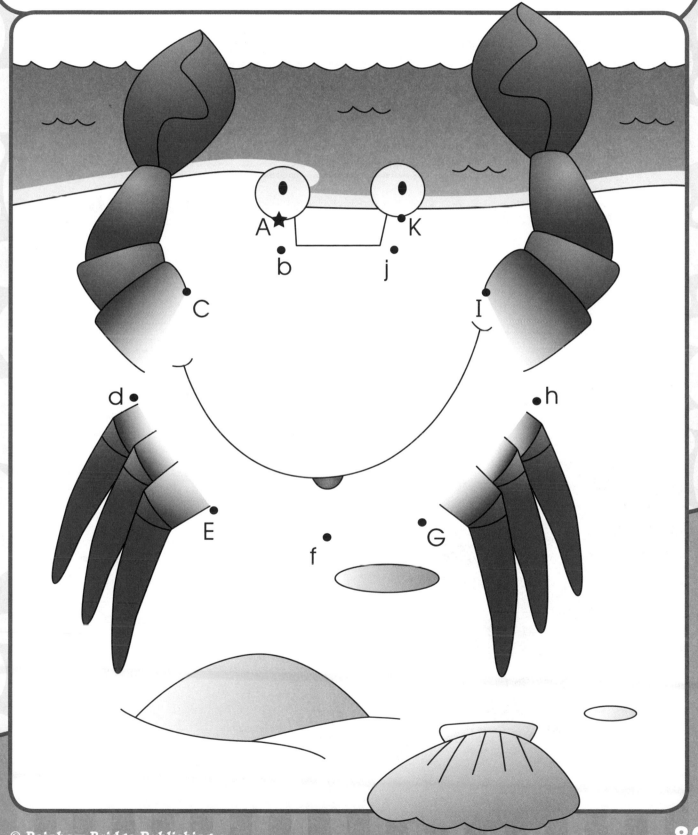

Circle the words hidden in the puzzle.

Word Bank

ant	apple	address
aunt	air	april

b y r l g g s j
j j a i r s f t
l r v a e e n q
o f a r p a k v
b o d p c p s z
w d a x r n l c
a a u n t i w e
b j x j n p l k

© Rainbow Bridge Publishing

Connect the dots from **a** to **k**. Start at the ★.
Color the picture.

© Rainbow Bridge Publishing

Connect the dots from **1** to **20**. Start at the ★.
Color the picture.

© Rainbow Bridge Publishing

Cut out each sailboat. Paste the sailboats on the picture.

cut ✂

© Rainbow Bridge Publishing

Connect the dots from **a** to **p**. Start at the ★.
Color the picture.

Connect the dots from **1** to **20**. Start at the ★.
Color the picture.

8 ●

● 9

16 ●

17 ●

7 ●

● 10

15 ●

6 ●

● 11

14 ●

● 18

5 ●

12 ●

13 ●

● 19

4 ●

3 ●

2 ●

1 ★━━━━━━━━● 20

© Rainbow Bridge Publishing

Connect the dots from **1** to **20**. Start at the ★.
Color the picture.

Circle the words hidden in the puzzle.

Word Bank

stable	barn	tractor
fence	farmer	crop

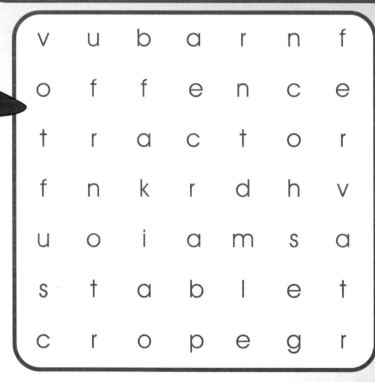

v u b a r n f
o f f e n c e
t r a c t o r
f n k r d h v
u o i a m s a
s t a b l e t
c r o p e g r

© Rainbow Bridge Publishing

Cut out each kite. Paste the kites on the picture.

cut

© Rainbow Bridge Publishing

Connect the dots from **1** to **20**. Start at the ★.
Color the picture.

Bubble
Bath

SOAP

3

2

4

1

20

5

19

18

6

9

17

16

8

7

10

15

11

14

12

13

Connect the dots from **A** to **P**. Start at the ★.
Color the picture.

© Rainbow Bridge Publishing

Color each space to find the hidden picture.

□ = dark blue   △ = light blue   ○ = yellow

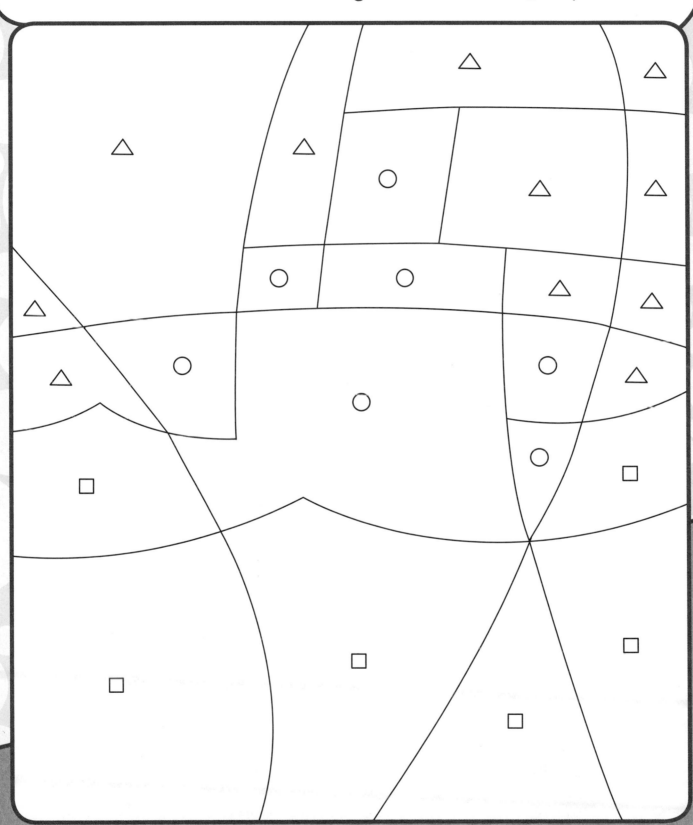

© Rainbow Bridge Publishing

Connect the dots from **1** to **20**. Start at the ★.
Color the picture.

11
10
9
8
13
7
12
6
15
14
5
16
17
4
2 3
18 19
1
20

© Rainbow Bridge Publishing

Cut out the puzzle pieces. Put the puzzle together.

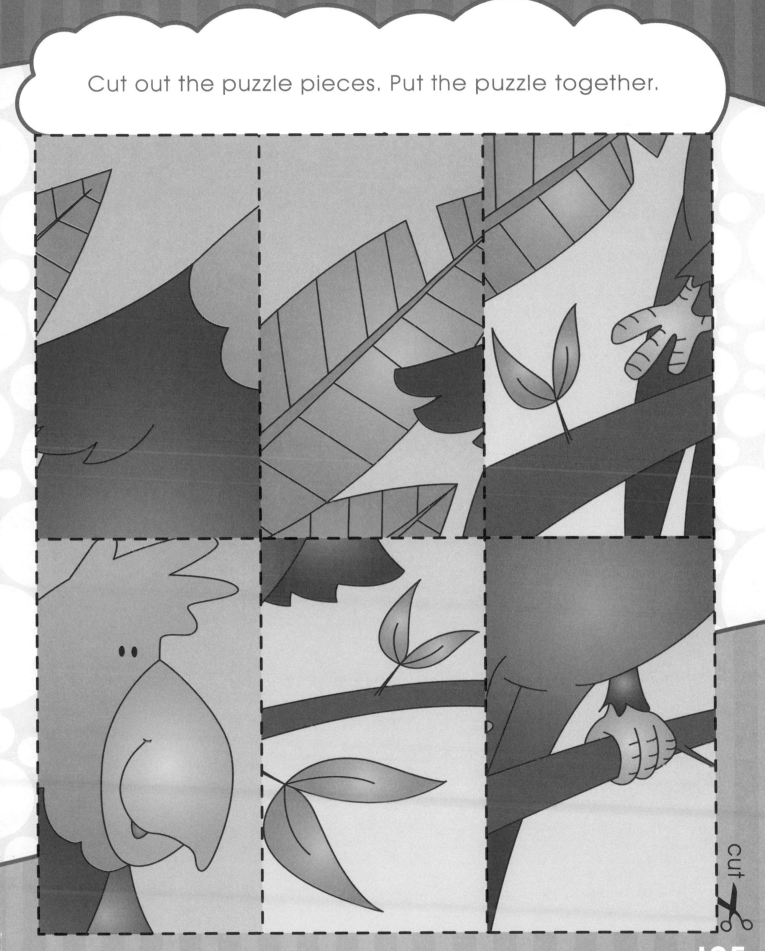

cut

Connect the dots from **1** to **20**. Start at the ★.
Color the picture.

Circle the words hidden in the puzzle.

Word Bank

bicycle	balloon	truck
airplane	bus	train
car	motorcycle	boat

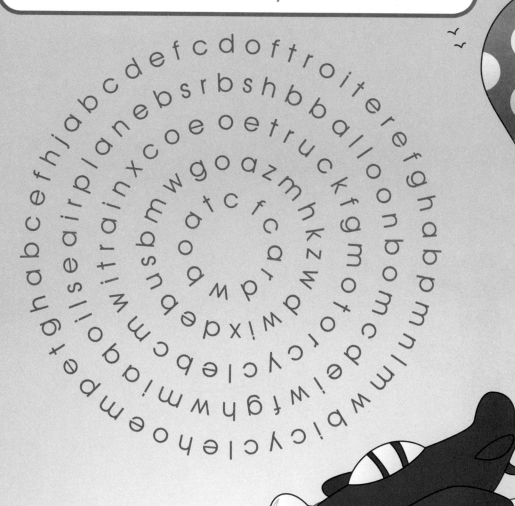

© Rainbow Bridge Publishing

Connect the dots from **A** to **p**. Start at the ★.
Color the picture.

Connect the dots from **a** to **p**. Start at the ★.
Color the picture.

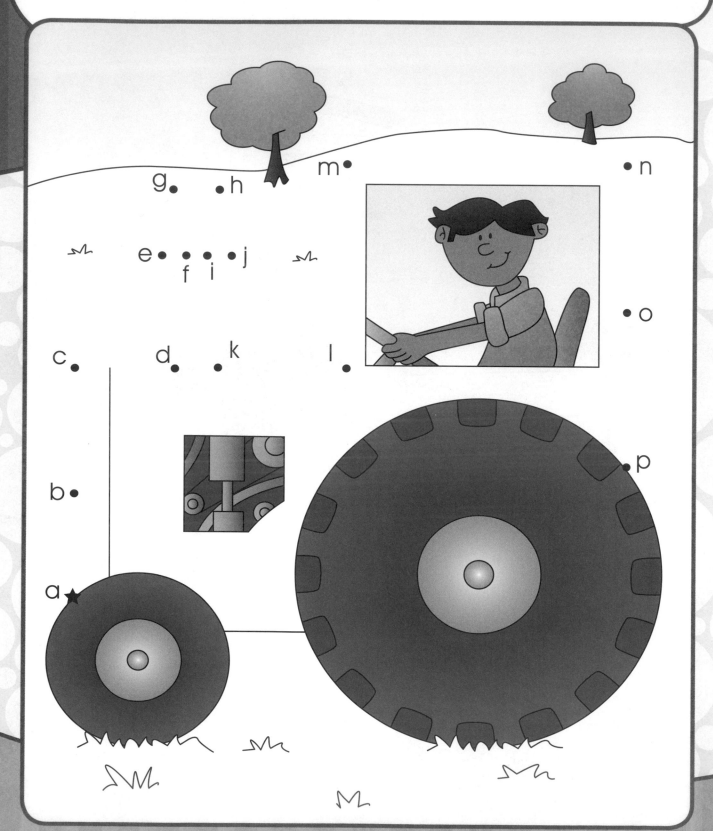

© Rainbow Bridge Publishing

Cut out each circle. Paste the circles on the picture.

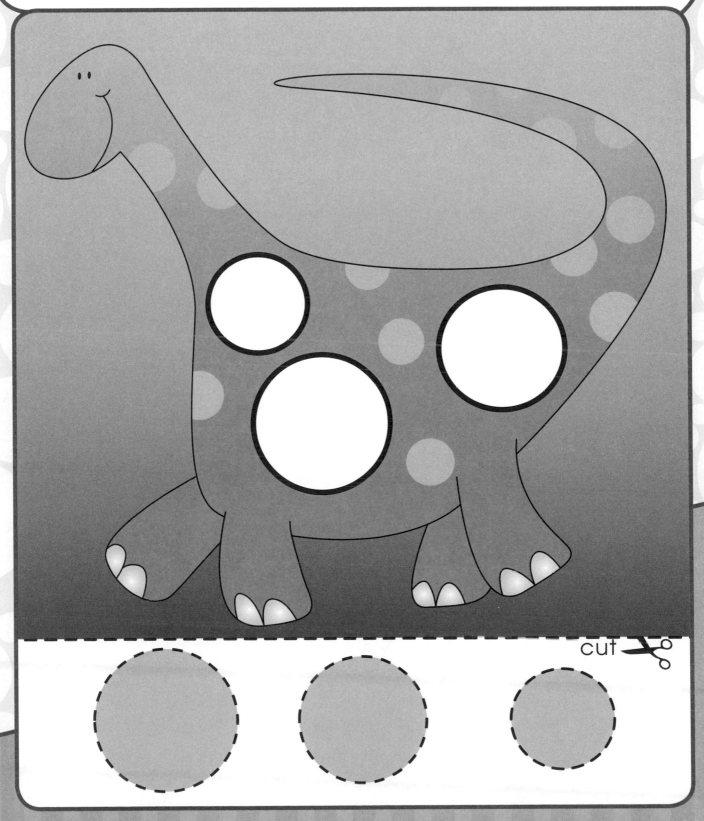

cut

© Rainbow Bridge Publishing

Connect the dots from **A** to **P**. Start at the ★.
Color the picture.

Connect the dots from **1** to **20**. Start at the ★.
Color the picture.

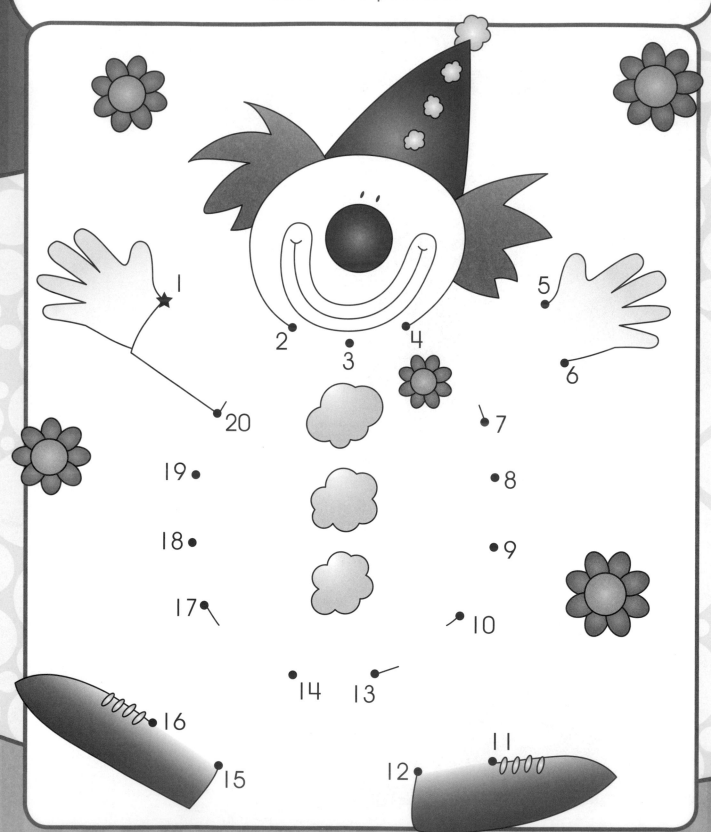

© Rainbow Bridge Publishing

Draw a line to help the dog find the bone.

Connect the dots from **1** to **25**. Start at the ★.
Color the picture.

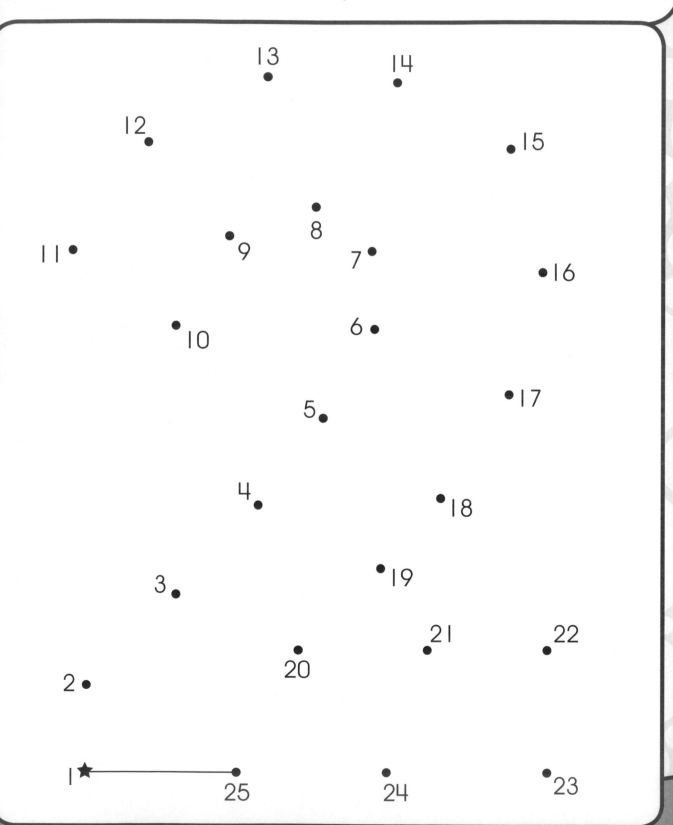

© Rainbow Bridge Publishing

Cut out each balloon. Paste the balloons on the picture.

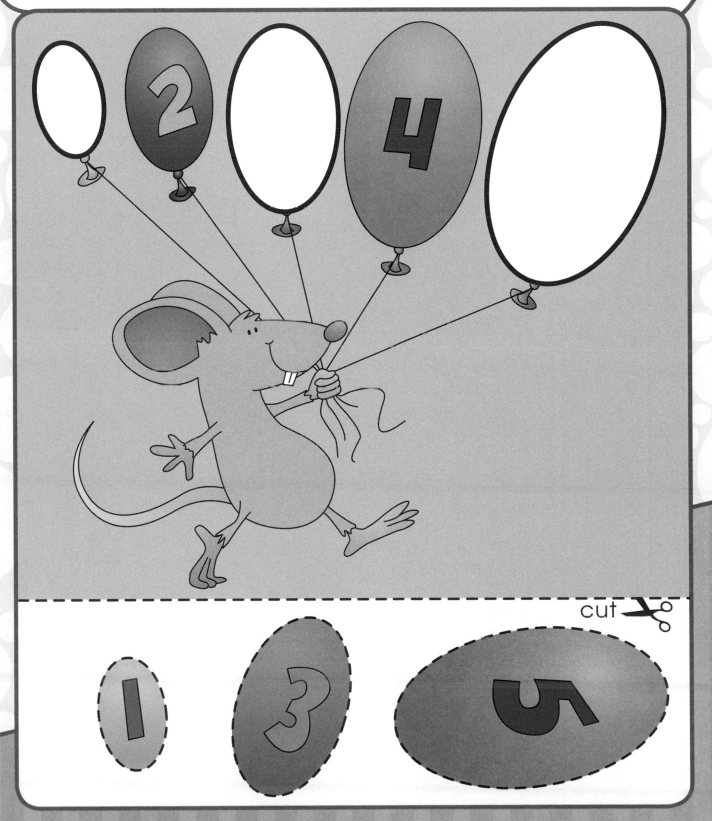

cut ✂

© Rainbow Bridge Publishing

Connect the dots from **A** to **p**. Start at the ★.
Color the picture.

Connect the dots from **A** to **P**. Start at the ★.
Color the picture.

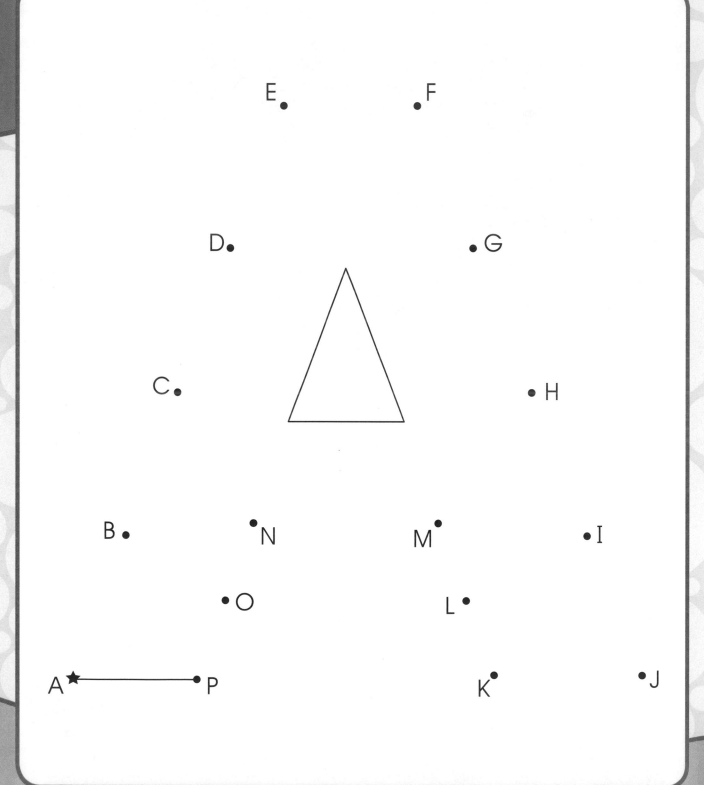

© Rainbow Bridge Publishing

Circle the words hidden in the puzzle.

Word Bank

sun	stars	moon
earth	rocket	alien

s	x	o	n	j	r	u	v
t	p	r	o	c	k	e	t
a	s	u	n	p	c	a	l
r	x	h	t	w	y	l	f
s	e	a	r	t	h	i	p
l	a	a	e	q	x	e	b
r	d	e	m	o	o	n	b
m	h	g	c	b	q	o	l

© Rainbow Bridge Publishing

Connect the dots from **A** to **U**. Start at the ★.
Color the picture.

D.   E.   F.   G

J.   I.   .H

C.

K.   L.   M.

P.   O.   N.

B.

Q.   R.   S.

A★————————•   •T
            U

© Rainbow Bridge Publishing

Cut out each fish. Paste the fish on the picture.

cut ✂

© Rainbow Bridge Publishing

123

Connect the dots from **a** to **u**. Start at the ★.
Color the picture.

Circle the words hidden in the puzzle.

Word Bank

zero	one	two	three	four
five	six	seven	eight	nine

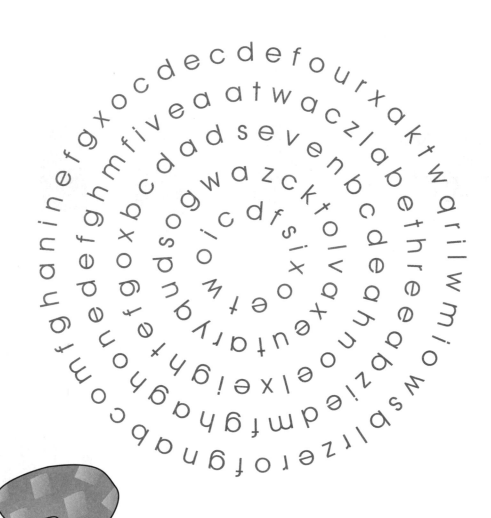

© Rainbow Bridge Publishing

Connect the dots from **1** to **25**. Start at the ★.
Color the picture.

Connect the dots from **a** to **u**. Start at the ★. Color the picture.

© Rainbow Bridge Publishing

Cut out the puzzle pieces. Put the puzzle together.

© Rainbow Bridge Publishing

cut

129

Color each space to find the hidden picture.

G = green   P = pink   R = red

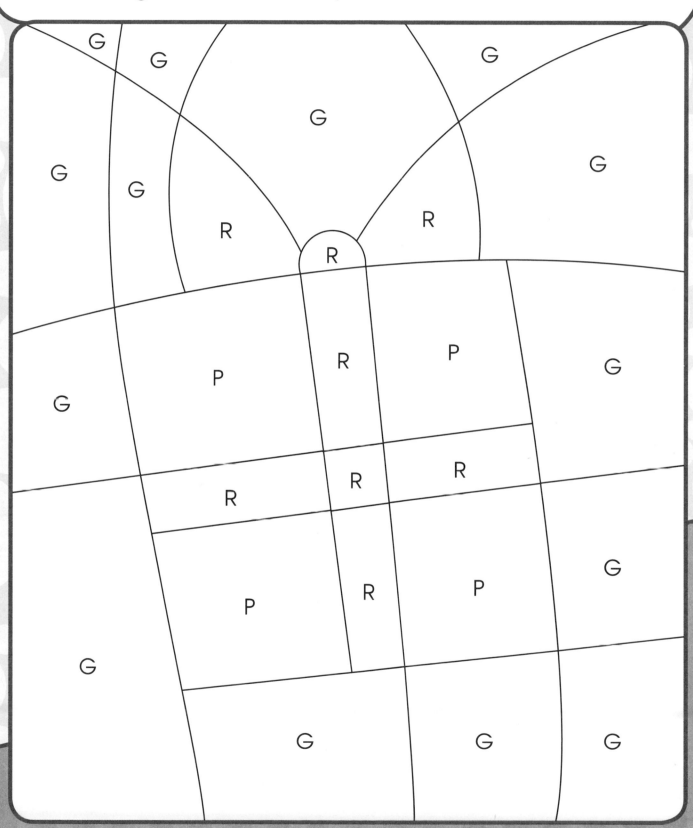

Connect the dots from **1** to **25**. Start at the ★.
Color the picture.

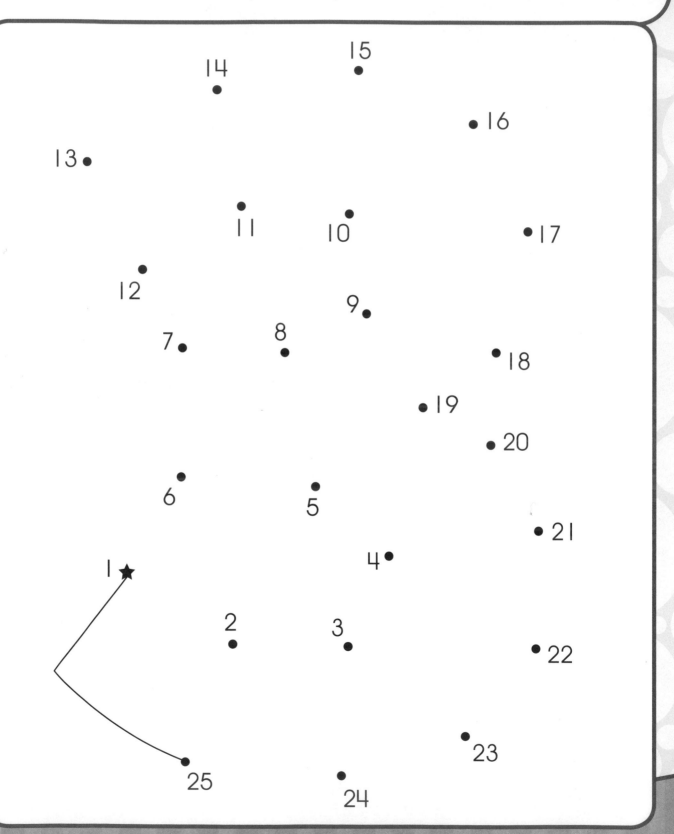

© Rainbow Bridge Publishing

Connect the dots from **A** to **U**. Start at the ★.
Color the picture.

Connect the dots from **A** to **U**. Start at the ★.
Color the picture.

D

E

K

L

F

J

C

M

S

G   I

T

R

H

N

B

U

Q

★
A

P

O

© Rainbow Bridge Publishing

Cut out each hot air balloon. Paste the hot air balloons on the picture.

cut

Circle the words hidden in the puzzle.

Word Bank

arm	leg	head	finger
toe	knee	elbow	

```
x  o  f  u  j  m  x  f
r  e  s  i  o  g  r  l
j  p  l  g  n  b  k  l
c  e  a  b  y  g  n  e
a  i  s  h  o  z  e  g
i  r  k  e  t  w  e  r
y  z  m  a  d  o  j  u
w  u  u  d  b  n  e  a
```

© Rainbow Bridge Publishing

Connect the dots from 1 to 25. Start at the ★.
Color the picture.

© Rainbow Bridge Publishing

Connect the dots from **A** to **U**. Start at the ★.
Color the picture.

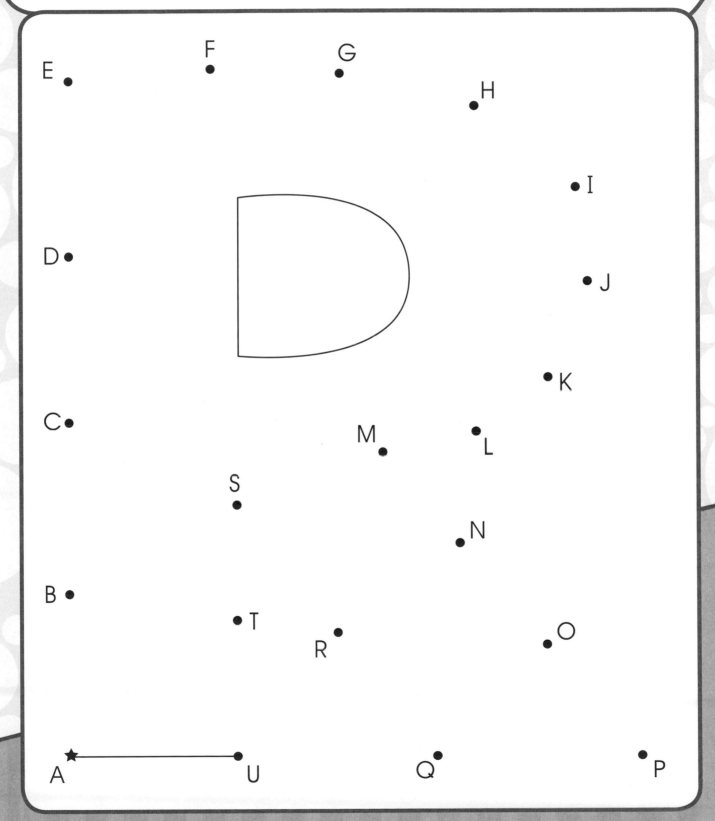

Connect the dots from **A** to **Z**. Start at the ★.
Color the picture.

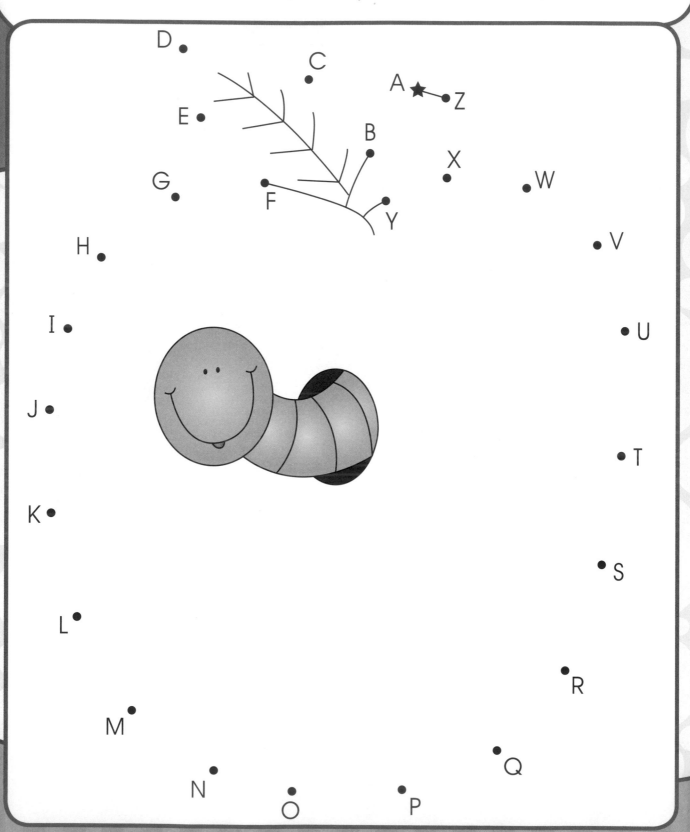

© Rainbow Bridge Publishing

Cut out each object. Paste the objects on the picture.

cut ✂

© Rainbow Bridge Publishing

Use a different color crayon to trace each line.
Who owns the dog?

© Rainbow Bridge Publishing

Connect the dots from **1** to **25**. Start at the ★.
Color the picture.

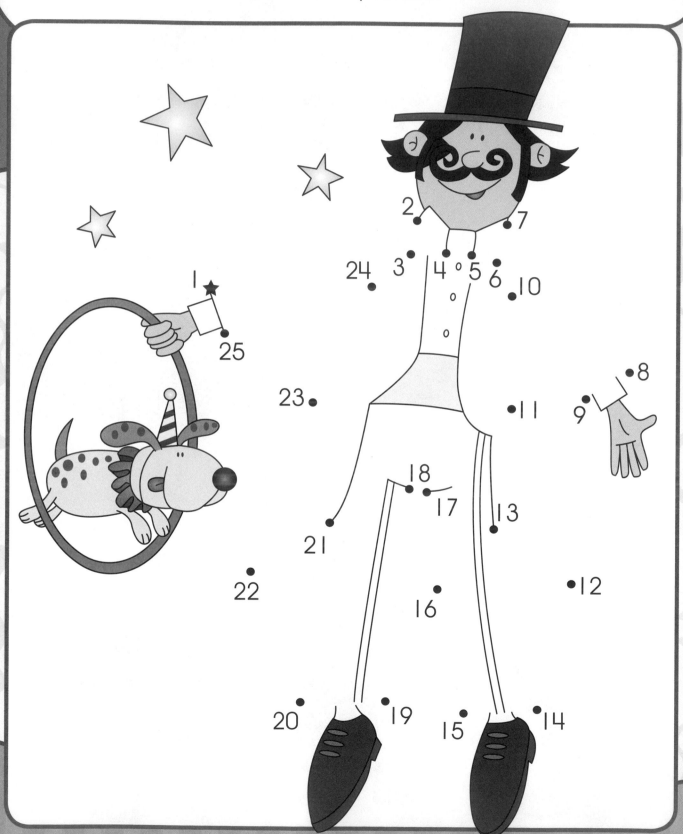

© Rainbow Bridge Publishing

Connect the dots from **A** to **Z**. Start at the ★.
Color the picture.

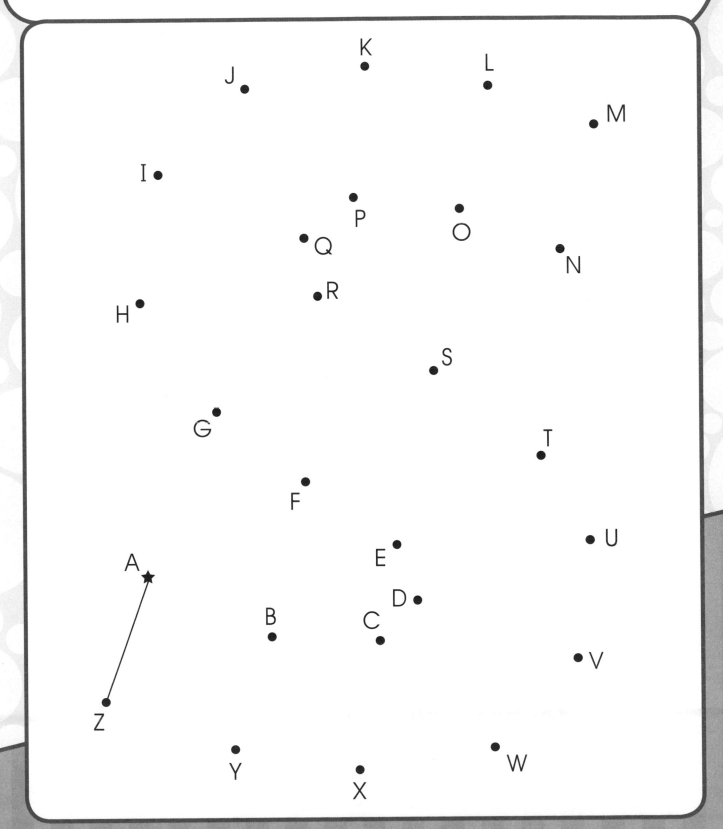

Connect the dots from **A** to **Z**. Start at the ★.
Color the picture.

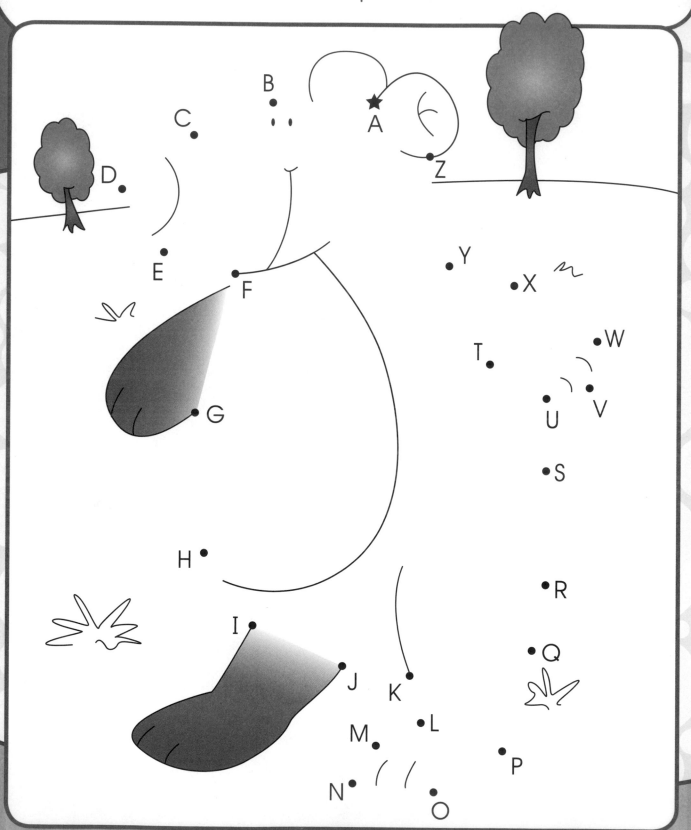

© Rainbow Bridge Publishing

Cut out the puzzle pieces. Put the puzzle together.

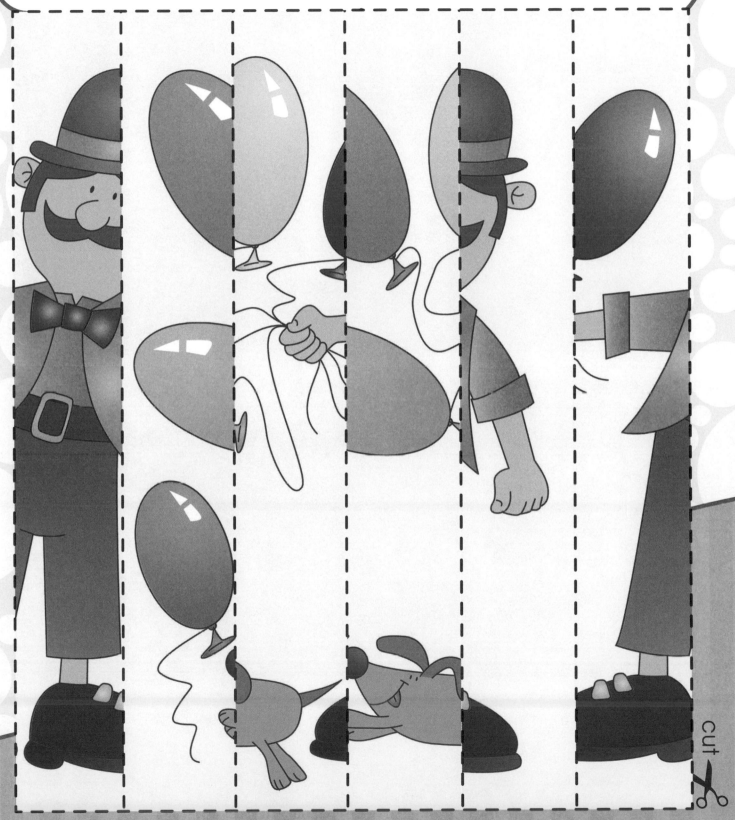

cut

Draw a line to help the socks find the the shoes.

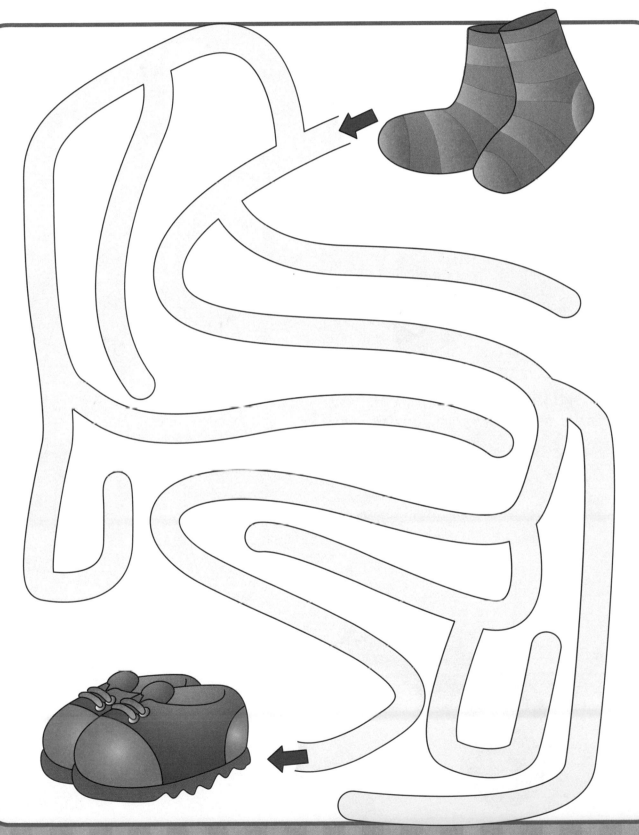

© Rainbow Bridge Publishing

Connect the dots from **A** to **Z**. Start at the ★.
Color the picture.

© Rainbow Bridge Publishing

Connect the dots from **1** to **25**. Start at the ★.
Color the picture.

11
12
13
14
10
16
15
9
17
18
19
8
6
7
5
20
1 ★
4
2
3
21
25
22
24
23

Color each space to find the hidden picture.

G = green   R = red   Y = yellow

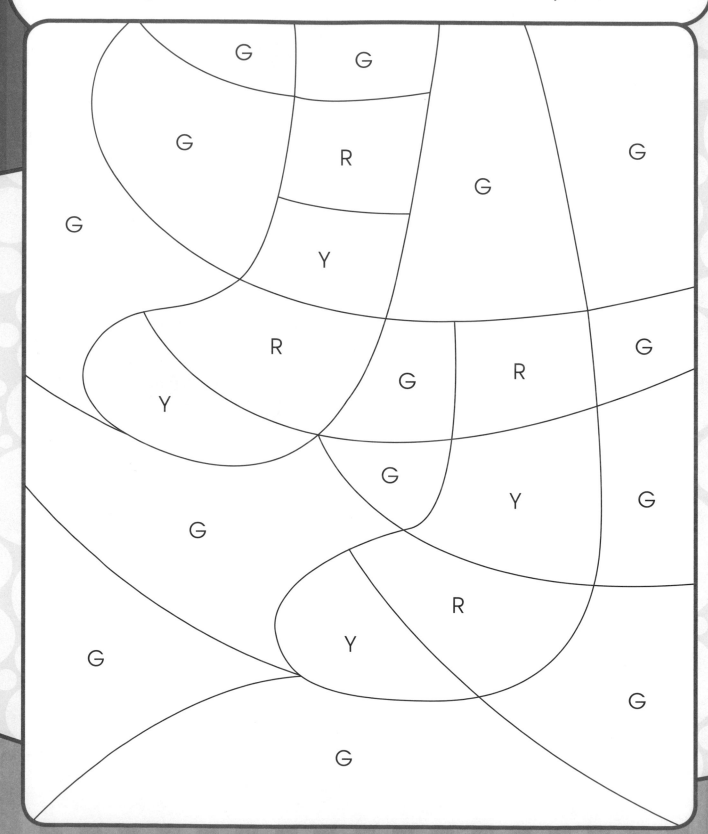

© Rainbow Bridge Publishing

Cut out the finger puppets.

cut

Connect the dots from **A** to **Z**. Start at the ★.
Color the picture.

Connect the dots from **1** to **30**. Start at the ★.
Color the picture.

1

30 2

6

26 5

3

29 27 7

4

28 8

25

24 9

23 10

22 16 11

21 15

17 12

20 14

18 13

19

© Rainbow Bridge Publishing

Connect the dots from **1** to **30**. Start at the ★.
Color the picture.

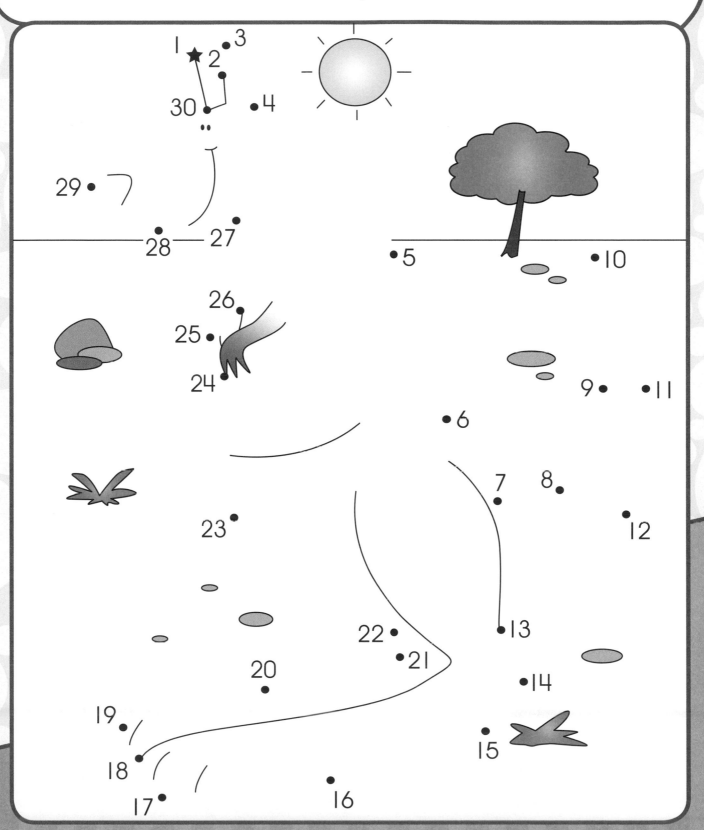

© Rainbow Bridge Publishing

Connect the dots from **A** to **Z**. Start at the ★.
Color the picture.

© Rainbow Bridge Publishing

Cut out each shape. Paste the shapes on the picture.

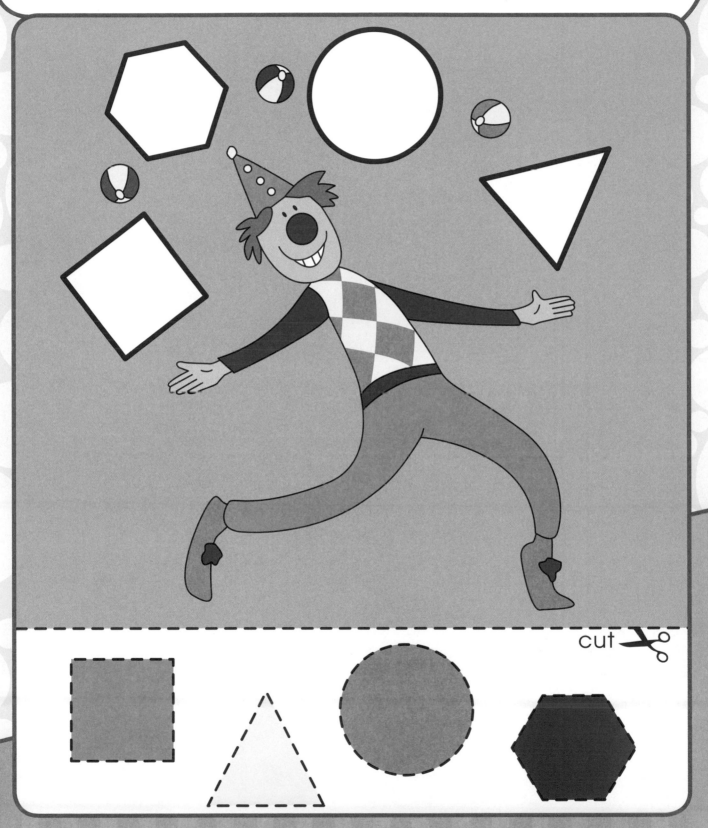

cut

© Rainbow Bridge Publishing

Draw a line to help the pencil find the pencil sharpener.

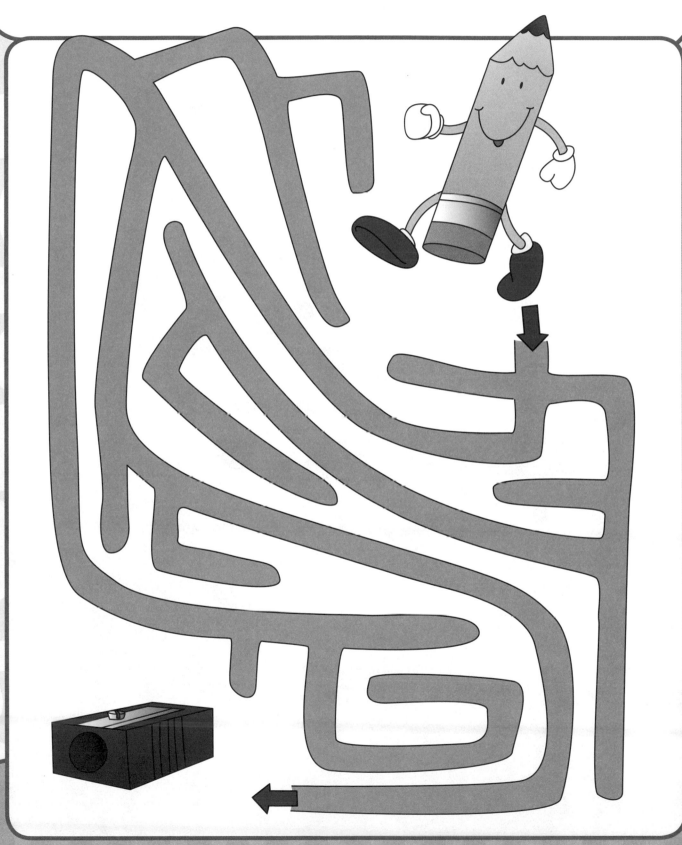

Connect the dots from **1** to **30**. Start at the ★.
Color the picture.

© Rainbow Bridge Publishing

Connect the dots from **A** to **Z**. Start at the ★. Color the picture.

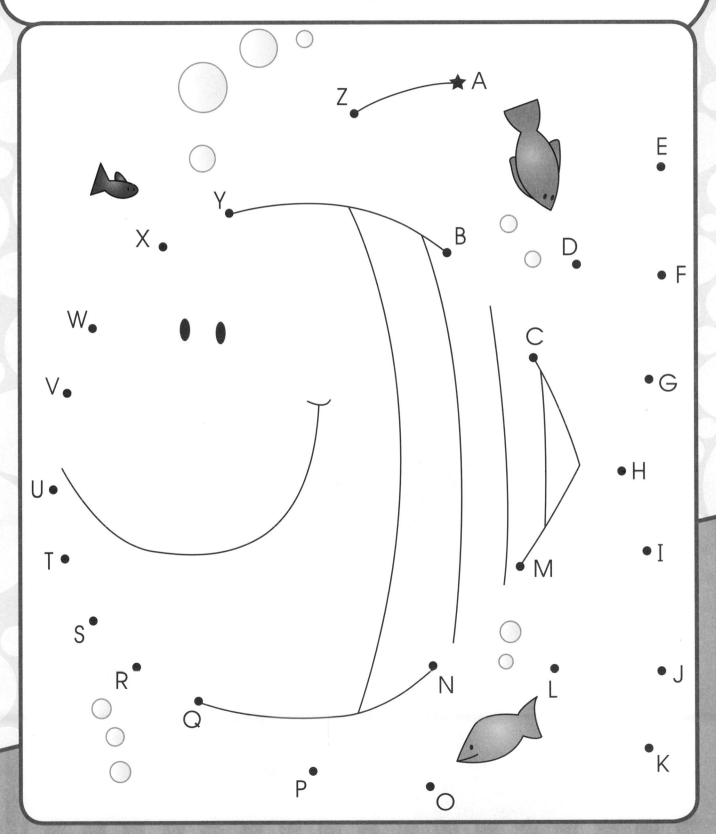

Connect the dots from **1** to **30**. Start at the ★.
Color the picture.

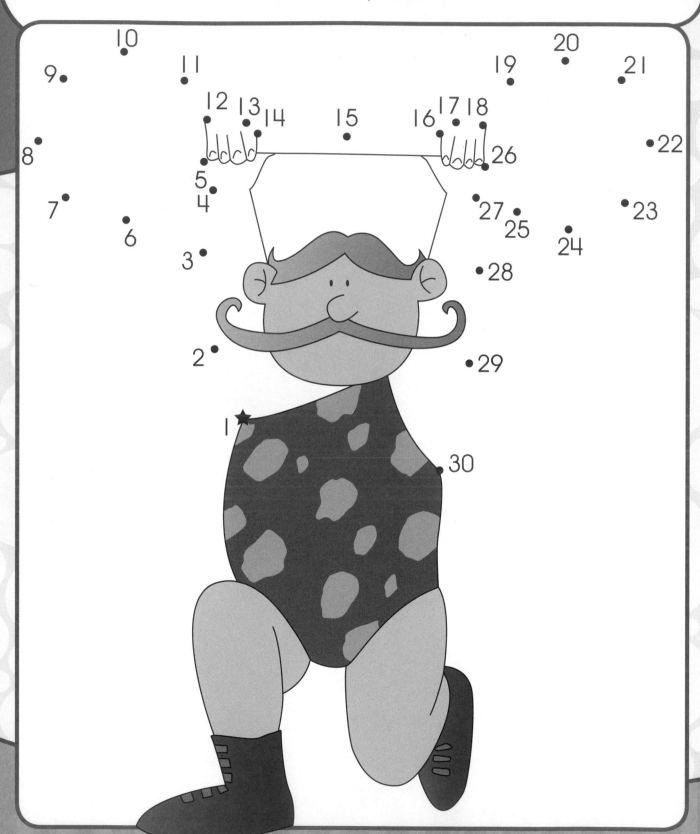

© Rainbow Bridge Publishing

Cut out the puzzle pieces. Put the puzzle together.

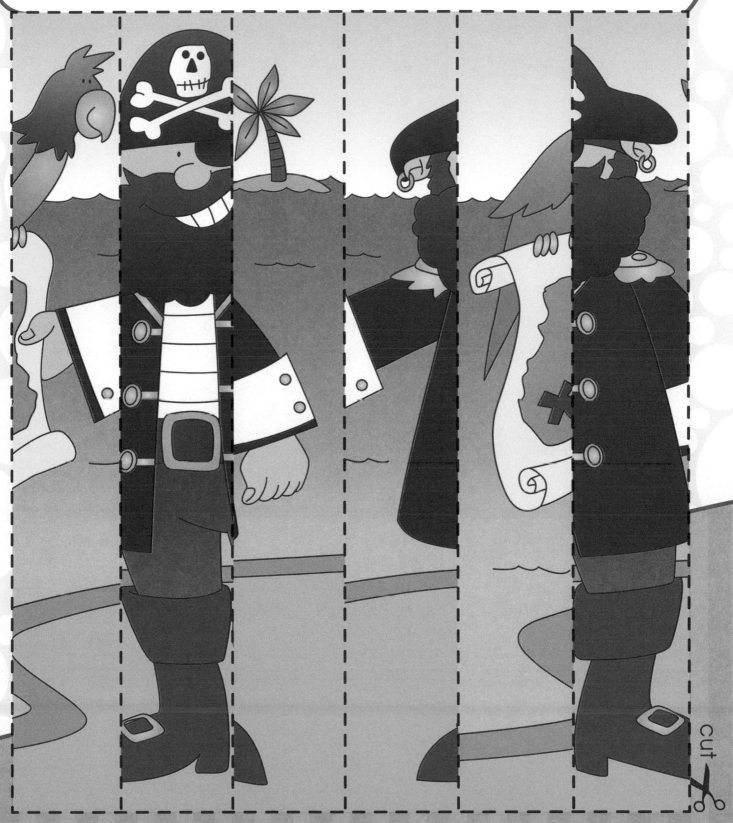

cut

Circle the words hidden in the puzzle.

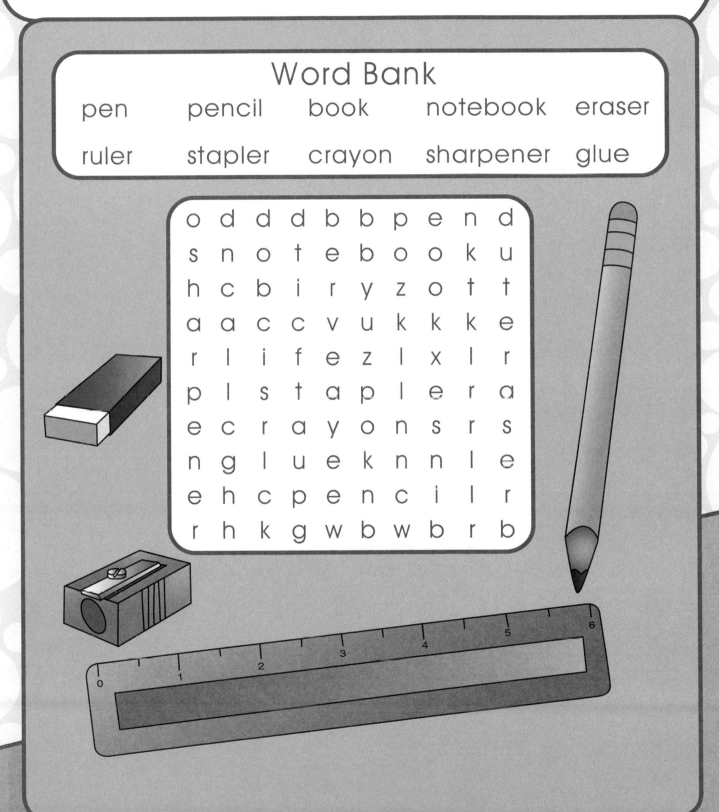

Word Bank

pen   pencil   book   notebook   eraser

ruler   stapler   crayon   sharpener   glue

```
o d d b b p e n d
s n o t e b o o k u
h c b i r y z o t t
a a c c v u k k e
r l i f e z l x l r
p l s t a p l e r a
e c r a y o n s r s
n g l u e k n n l e
e h c p e n c i l r
r h k g w b w b r b
```

Connect the dots from **1** to **30**. Start at the ★.
Color the picture.

© Rainbow Bridge Publishing

Connect the dots from **A** to **Z**. Start at the ★.
Color the picture.

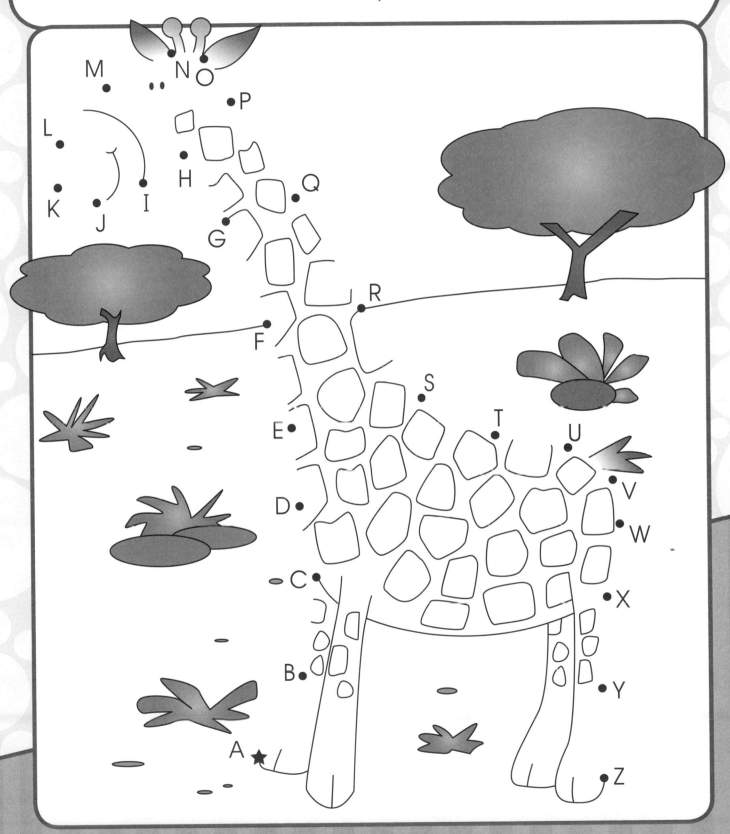

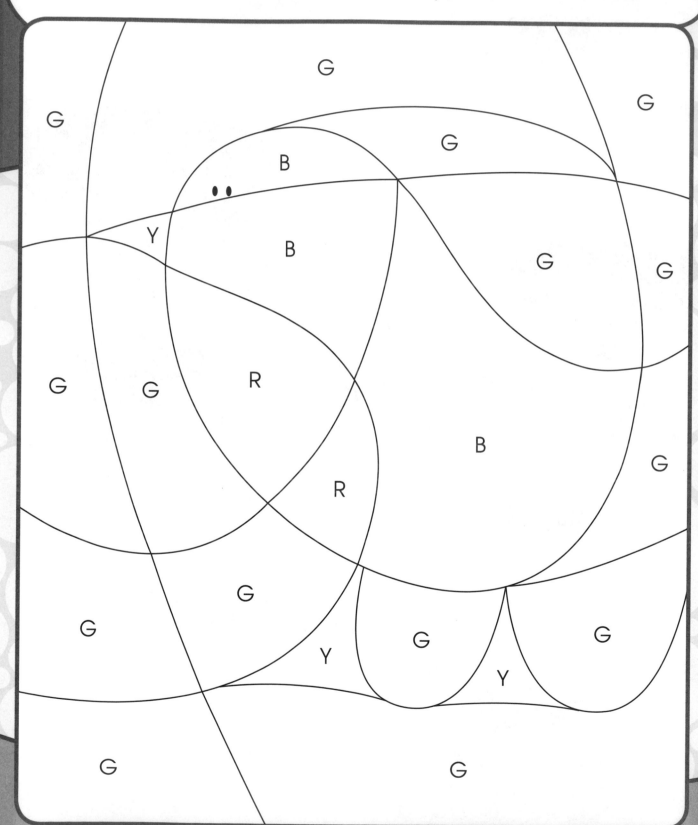

170

© Rainbow Bridge Publishing

Cut out each object. Paste the objects on the picture.

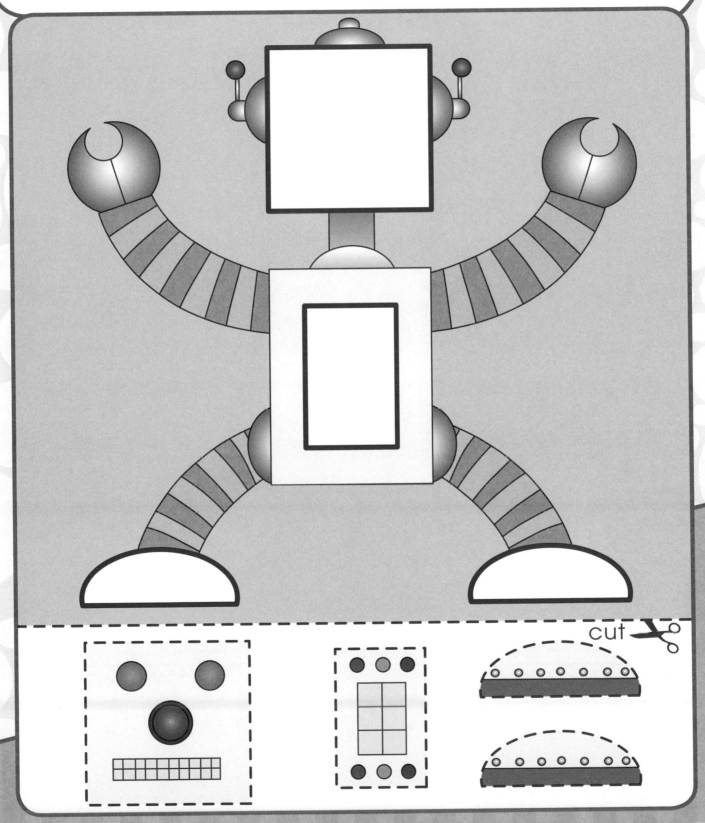

cut

© Rainbow Bridge Publishing

Connect the dots from **10** to **20**. Start at the ★.
Color the picture.

© Rainbow Bridge Publishing

173

Connect the dots from **A** to **Z**. Start at the ★.
Color the picture.

C   D   E   F   G   H

B

I

★ Z   J

A Z   K

Y   L

X   M

W   N

V   O

U   T   S   R   Q   P

© Rainbow Bridge Publishing

Connect the dots from **2** to **20**. Count by 2s.
Start at the ★. Color the picture.

© Rainbow Bridge Publishing

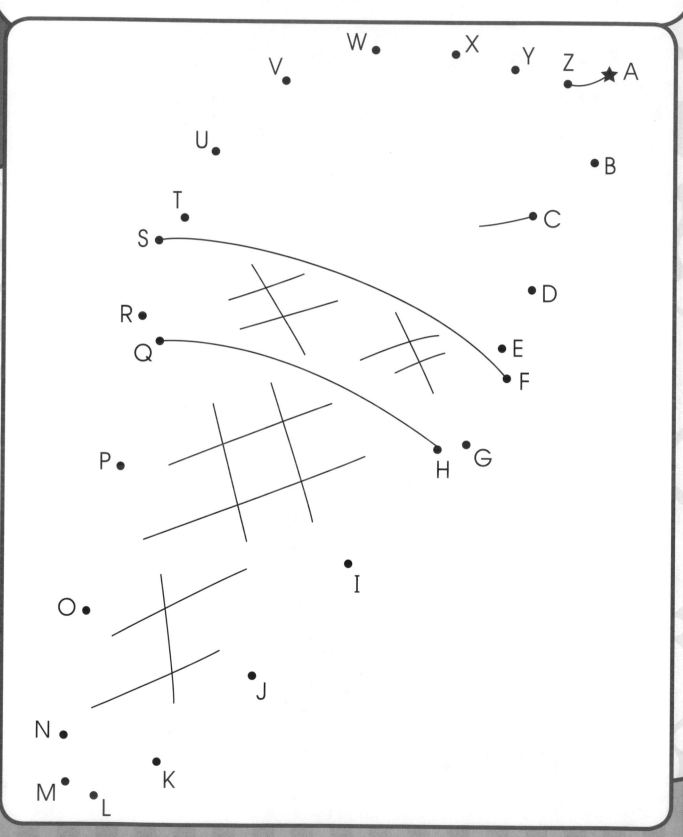

© Rainbow Bridge Publishing

Cut out the shoes and the mittens. Paste the shoes and the mittens on the picture.

cut ✂

© Rainbow Bridge Publishing

Look at the pictures. Write the words
to solve the crossword puzzle.

1. toad

2. horse

3. snake

4.elk

© Rainbow Bridge Publishing

Connect the dots from **2** to **20**. Count by 2s.
Start at the ★. Color the picture.

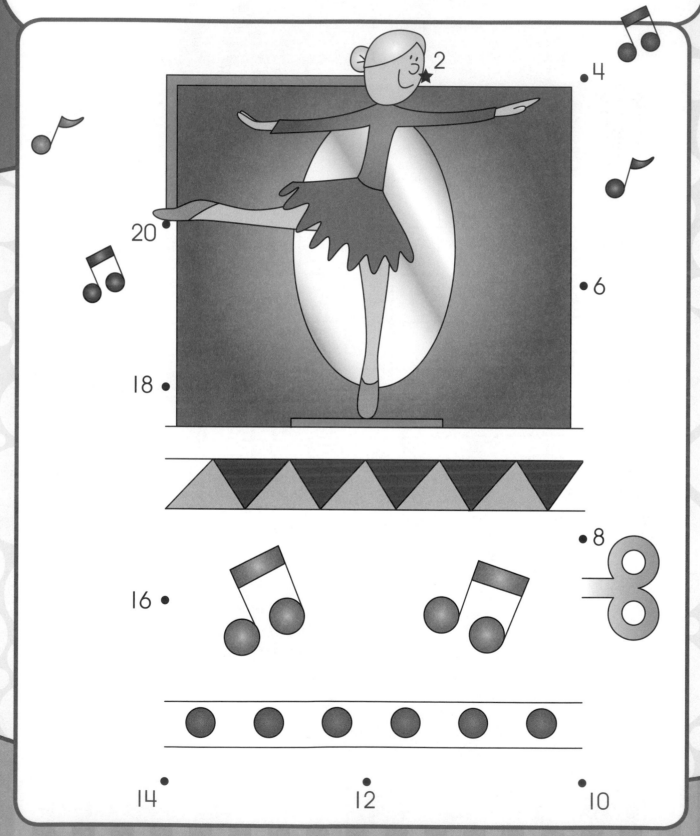

© Rainbow Bridge Publishing

Connect the dots from **A** to **Z**. Start at the ★.
Color the picture.

Look at the pictures. Write the words
to solve the crossword puzzle.

1. fork

2. spoon

3. knife

4. napkin

© Rainbow Bridge Publishing

Cut out the puzzle pieces. Put the puzzle together.

cut

Connect the dots from **A** to **Z**. Start at the ★.
Color the picture.

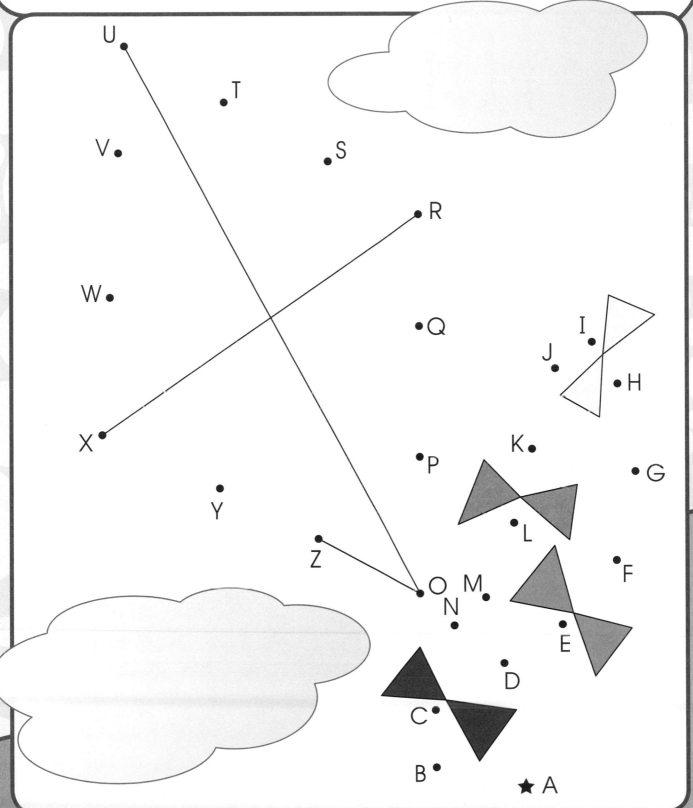

Connect the dots from **2** to **20**. Count by 2s.
Start at the ★. Color the picture.

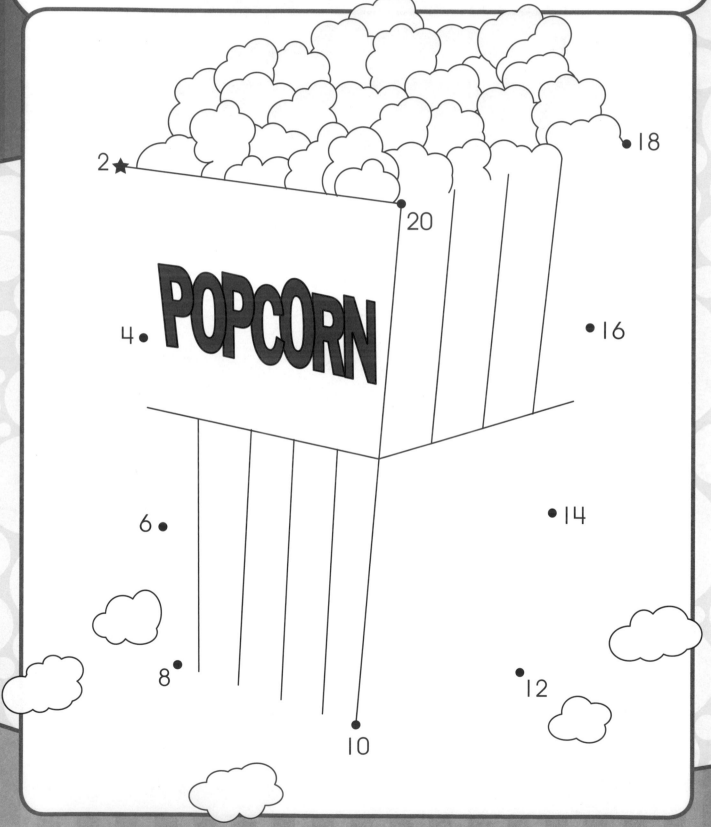

2 ★

•18

20

4•

POPCORN

•16

6•

•14

8•

•12

10

© Rainbow Bridge Publishing

Color each space to find the hidden picture.

B = blue   Y = yellow   R = red   O = orange

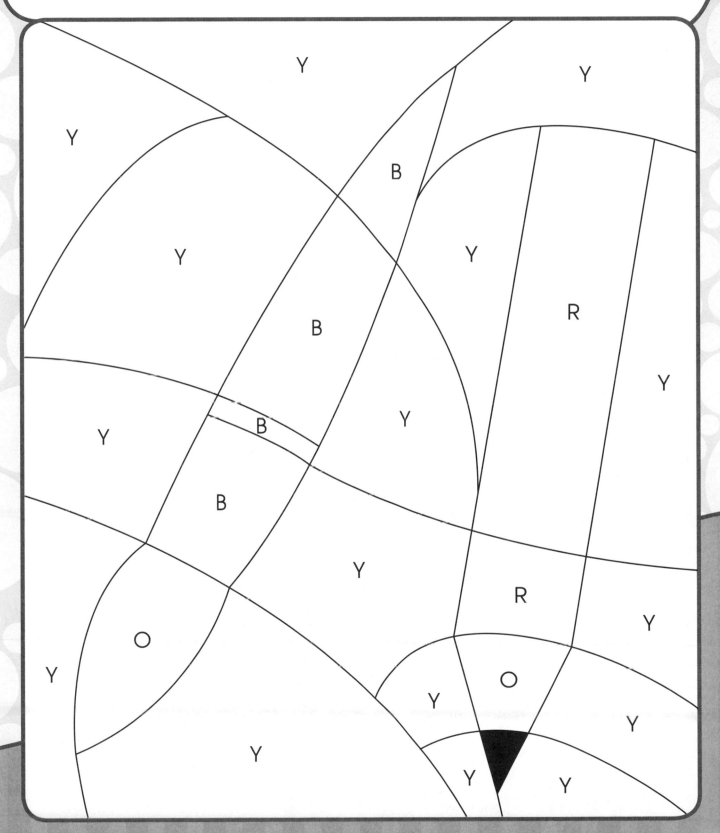

Finish the crossword puzzle by writing the missing letters.

Word Bank

sand   shells   crab

surf   wave   swim

s | w | |

w

s | | e | | | s

c | |

© Rainbow Bridge Publishing

Cut out each object. Tie each object with string.
Hang the objects as a mobile.

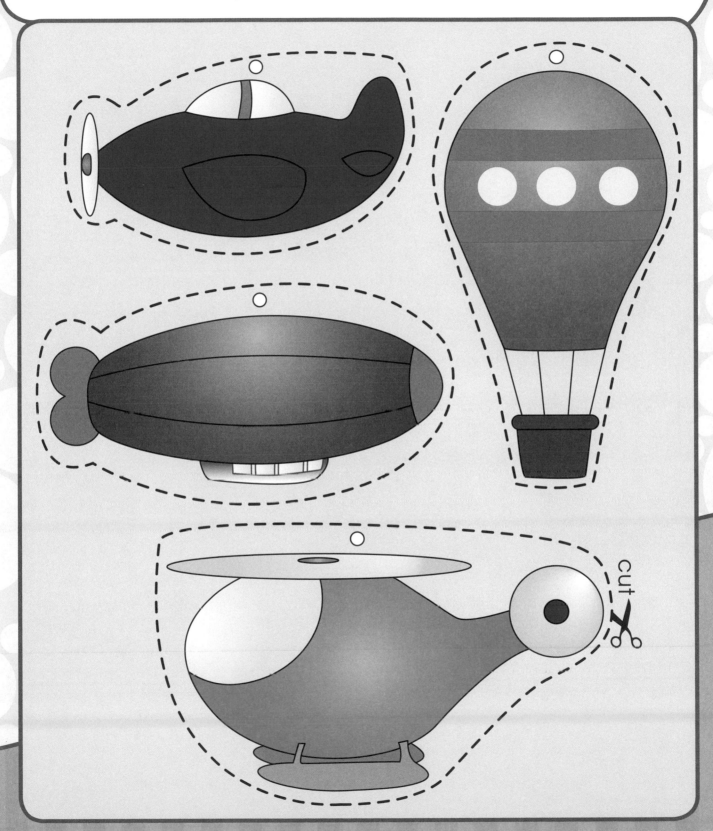

cut

© Rainbow Bridge Publishing

Connect the dots from **2** to **30**. Count by 2s.
Start at the ★. Color the picture.

Connect the dots from **A** to **Z**. Start at the ★.
Color the picture.

© Rainbow Bridge Publishing

Connect the dots from **2** to **30**. Count by 2s.
Start at the ★. Color the picture.

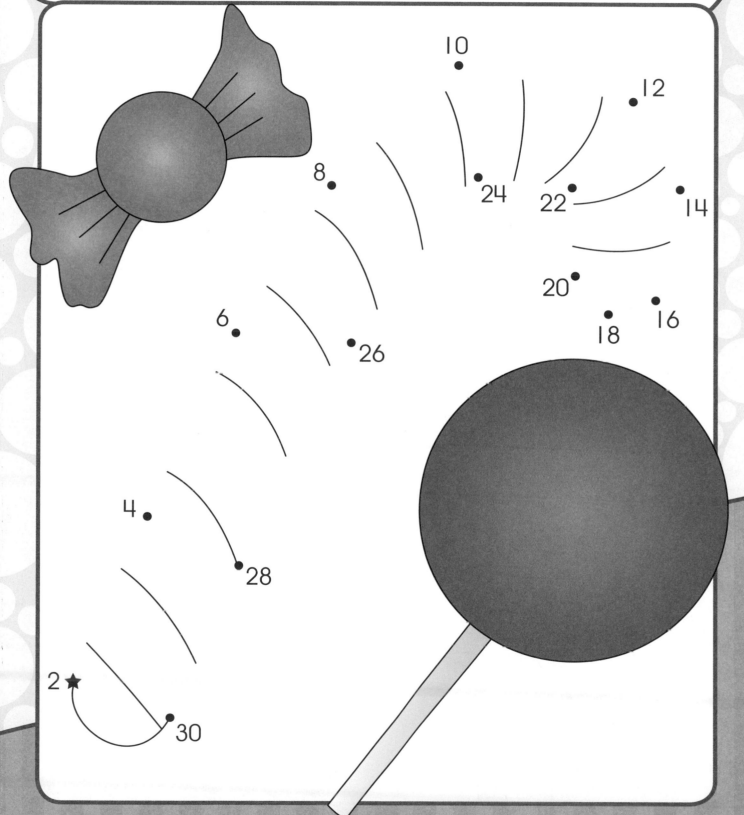

Connect the dots from **A** to **Z**. Start at the ★. Color the picture.

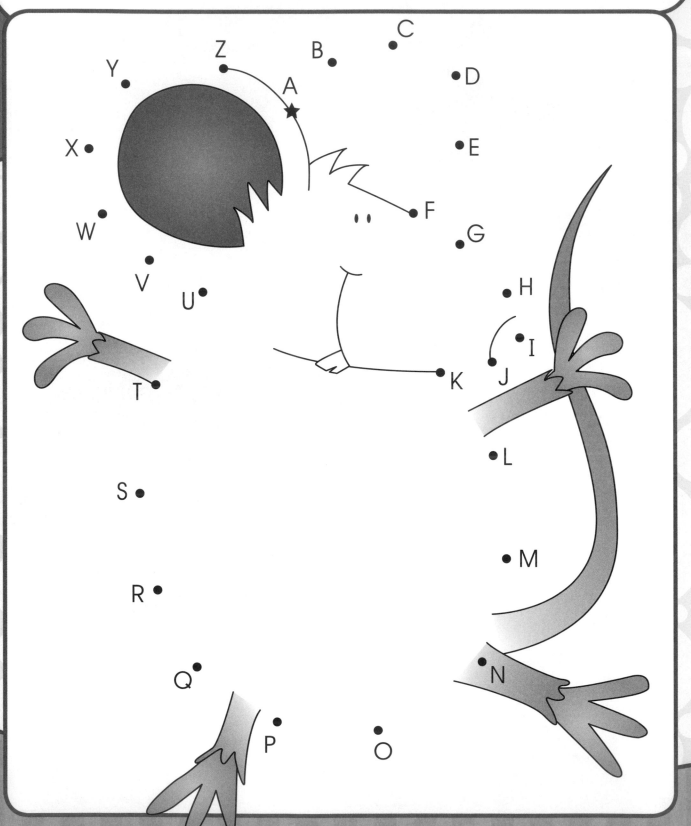

© Rainbow Bridge Publishing

Cut along the dotted lines. Fold along the solid lines to make the animals stand up.

cut

© Rainbow Bridge Publishing

Finish the crossword puzzle by writing the missing letters.

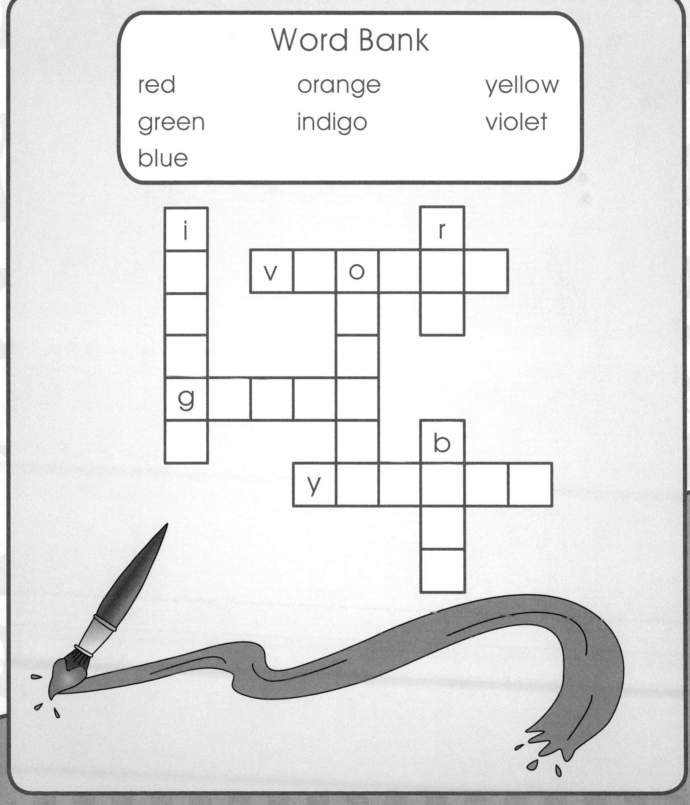

Word Bank

red	orange	yellow
green	indigo	violet
blue		

© Rainbow Bridge Publishing

Connect the dots from **2** to **30**. Count by 2s.
Start at the ★. Color the picture.

Connect the dots from **A** to **Z**. Start at the ★.
Color the picture.

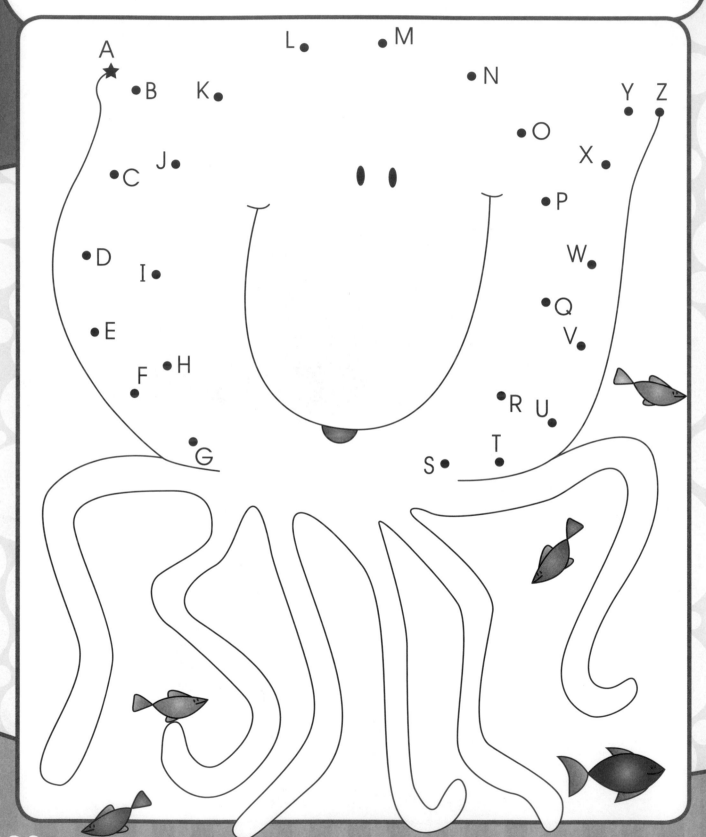

© Rainbow Bridge Publishing

Cut out the puzzle pieces. Put the puzzle together.

cut

Color each space to find the hidden picture.

A = yellow   B = red   C = blue   D = green   E = orange

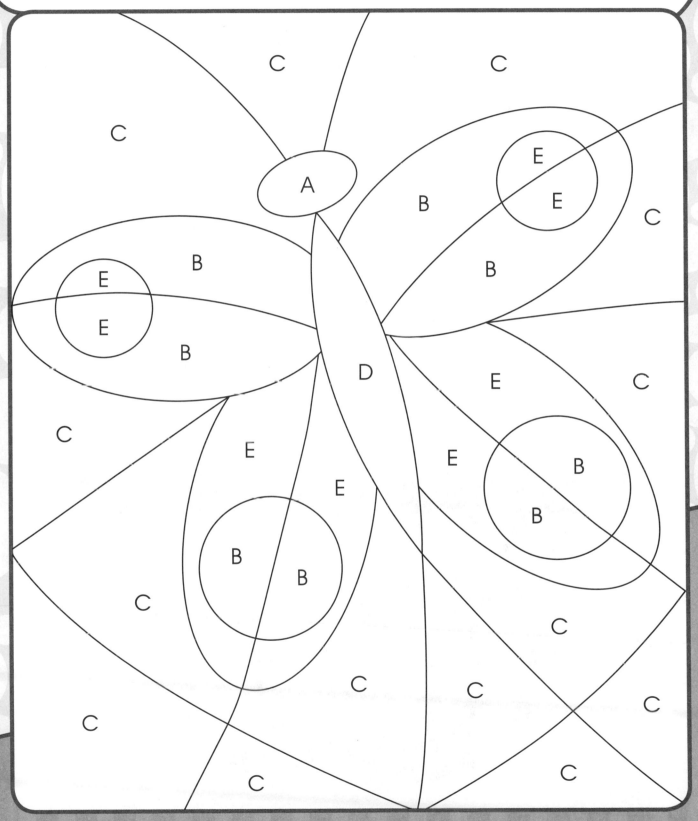

Connect the dots from **2** to **30**. Count by 2s.
Start at the ★. Color the picture.

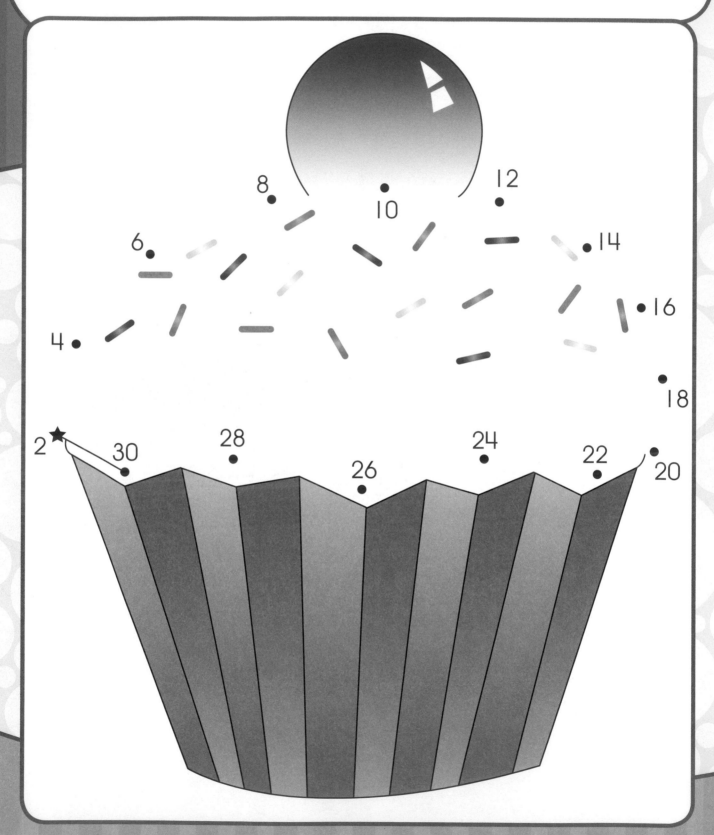

© Rainbow Bridge Publishing

Connect the dots from **A** to **Z**. Start at the ★.
Color the picture.

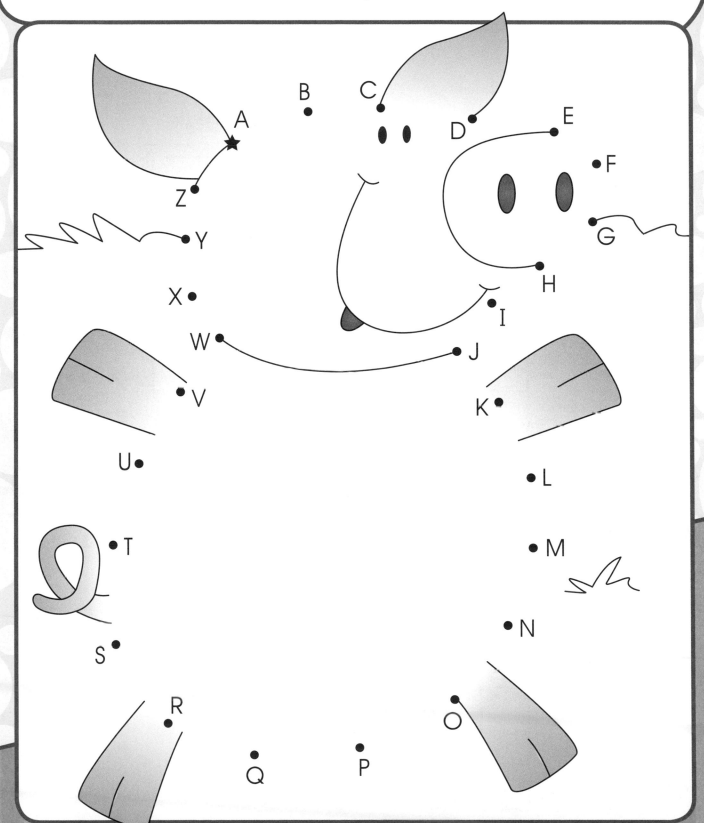

Finish the crossword puzzle by writing the missing letters.

Word Bank

icicles	ski	snowball	snowboard	skate
frost	ice	snow	snowmobile	

© Rainbow Bridge Publishing

Cut along the dotted lines. Fold along the solid lines.
Glue the tabs together.

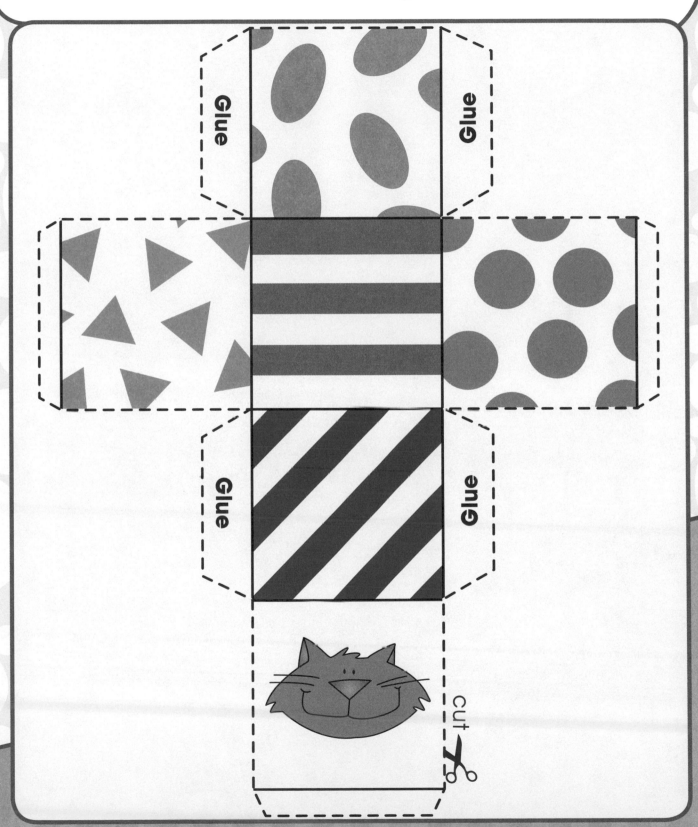

Connect the dots from **A** to **Z**. Start at the ★.
Color the picture.

© Rainbow Bridge Publishing

Connect the dots from **3** to **30**. Count by 3s.
Start at the ★. Color the picture.

15

21

18

12

24

9

6

30

27

3

© Rainbow Bridge Publishing

Connect the dots from **A** to **Z**. Start at the ★.
Color the picture.

A B C D E F G H I J K L M N O P Q R S T U V W X Y Z

Look at the pictures. Write the words and use the code to answer the question.

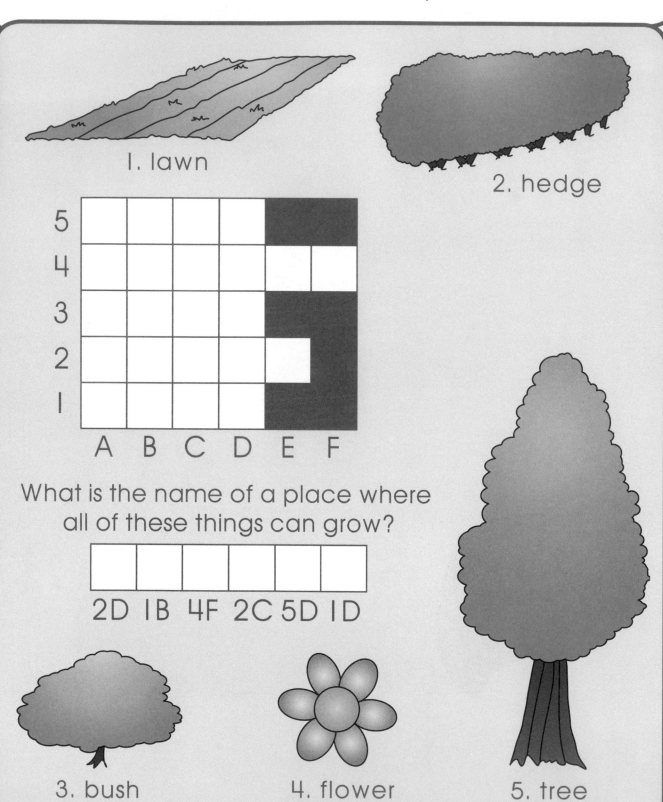

1. lawn

2. hedge

What is the name of a place where all of these things can grow?

2D IB 4F 2C 5D ID

3. bush

4. flower

5. tree

© Rainbow Bridge Publishing

Cut out the puzzle pieces. Put the puzzle together.

cut

Connect the dots from **A** to **Z**. Start at the ★.
Color the picture.

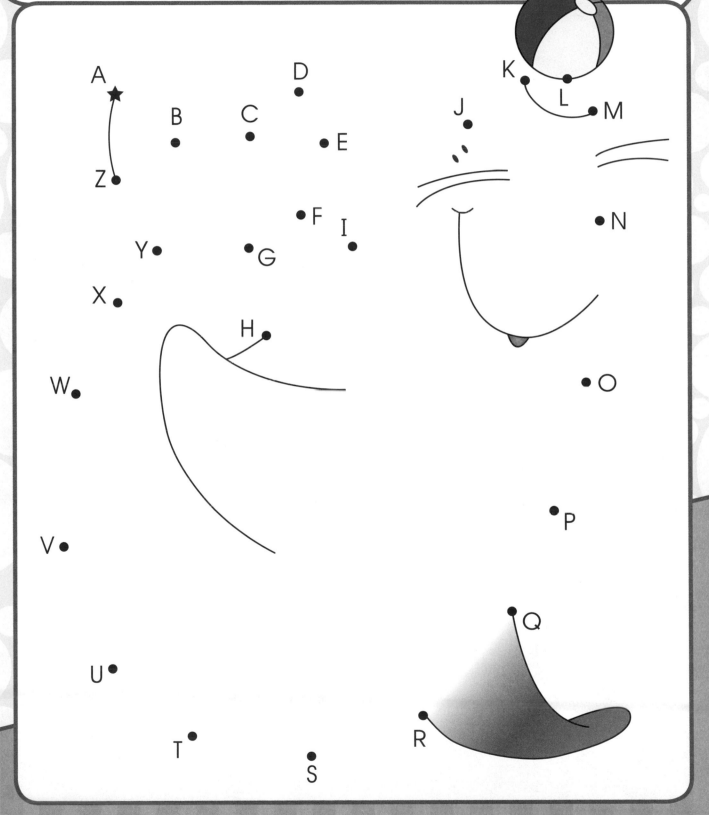

Draw a line to help the duck find her ducklings.

216

© Rainbow Bridge Publishing

Connect the dots from **3** to **30**. Count by 3s.
Start at the ★. Color the picture.

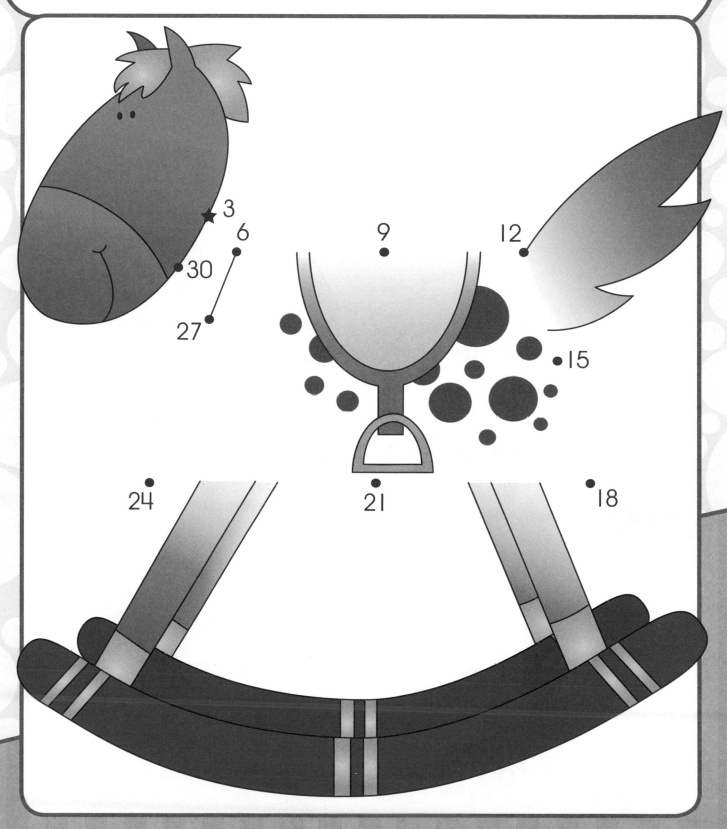

3

6

9

12

30

27

15

24

21

18

Connect the dots from **A** to **Z**. Start at the ★.
Color the picture.

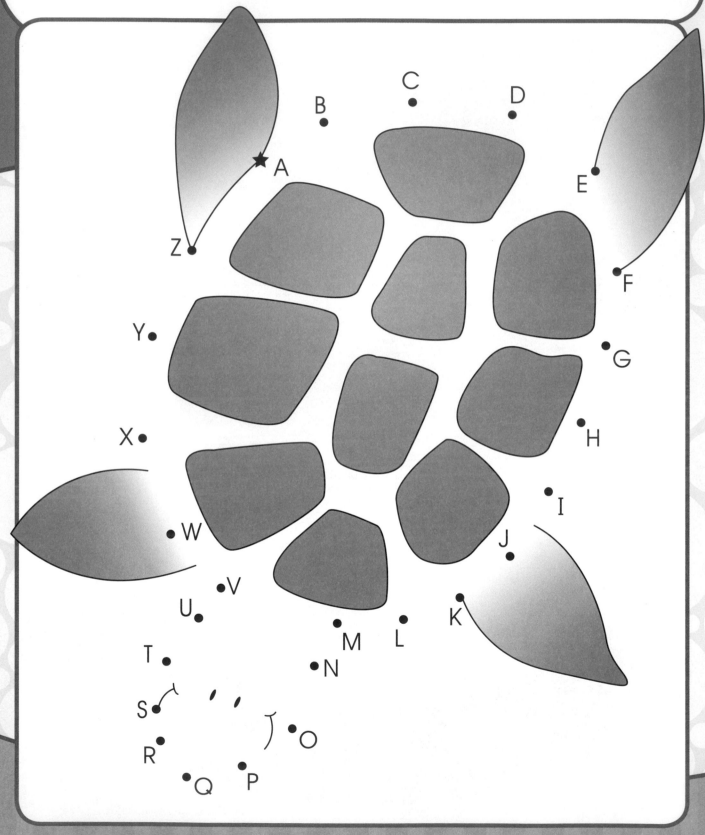

© Rainbow Bridge Publishing

Cut along the dotted lines. Fold along the solid lines to make the animals stand up.

cut

Look at the pictures. Write the words and use the code to answer the question.

1. socks

2. glove

3. jeans

4. sweater

5. shirt

What is a small space for storing clothes?

1C	2B	1B	5A	4F	5E

Connect the dots from **1** to **29**. Count by 2s.
Start at the ★. Color the picture.

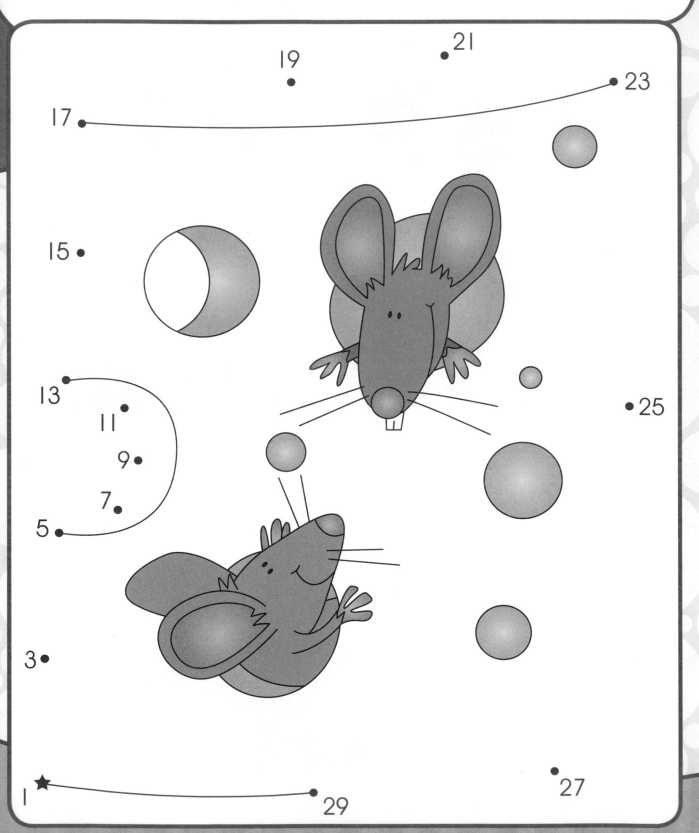

© Rainbow Bridge Publishing

Connect the dots from **A** to **Z**. Start at the ★.
Color the picture.

Look at the pictures. Write the words and use the code to answer the question.

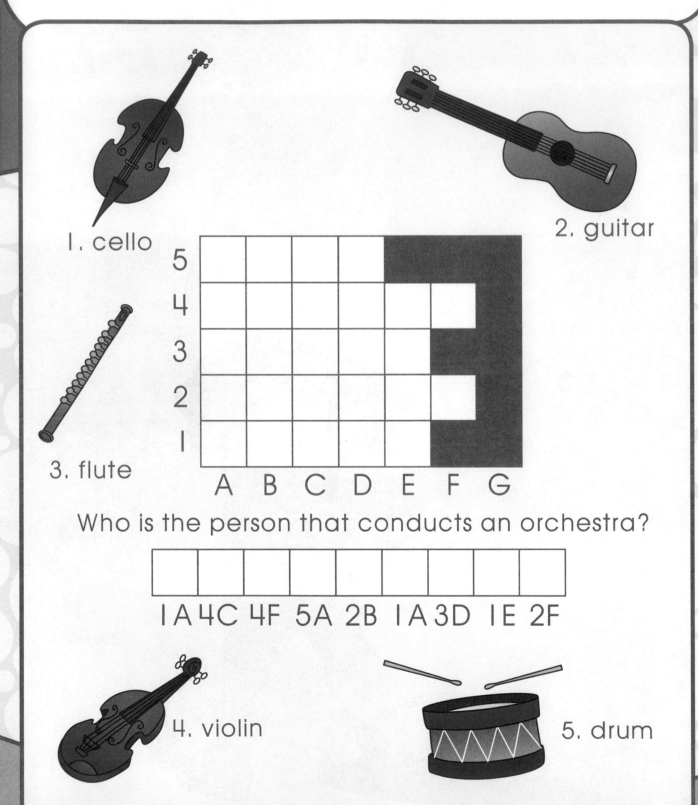

1. cello

2. guitar

3. flute

Who is the person that conducts an orchestra?

1A 4C 4F 5A 2B 1A 3D 1E 2F

4. violin

5. drum

© Rainbow Bridge Publishing

Cut out the puzzle pieces. Put the puzzle together.

Connect the dots from **A** to **Z**. Start at the ★.
Color the picture.

Draw a line to help the flower find the flowerpot.

© Rainbow Bridge Publishing

Connect the dots from **1** to **29**. Count by 2s.
Start at the ★. Color the picture.

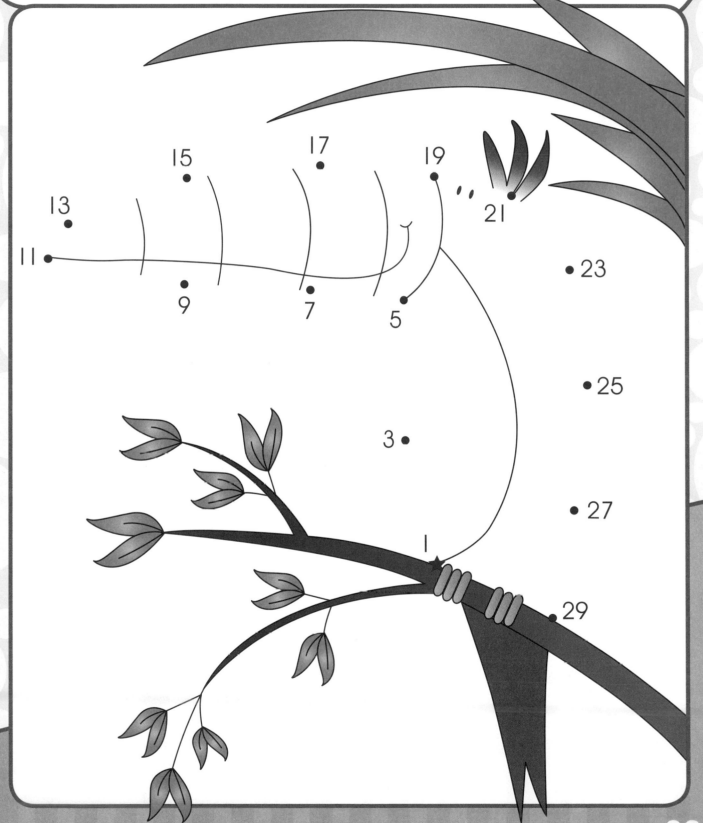

Connect the dots from **A** to **Z**. Start at the ★.
Color the picture.

230

© Rainbow Bridge Publishing

Cut along the dotted lines. Fold the card along the solid line. Place the candles in the slits on top of the card.

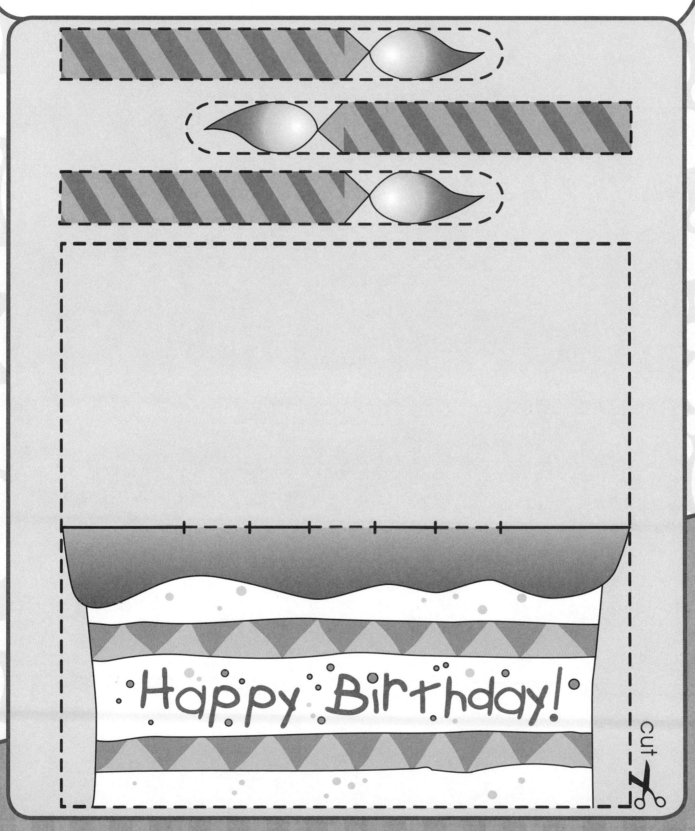

Happy Birthday!

cut

© Rainbow Bridge Publishing

Match the letters in the code to the numbers. Use the code to answer the question.

What is the name of an animal that has black and white stripes?

___ ___ ___ ___ ___
6   11   8   24   7

© Rainbow Bridge Publishing

Connect the dots from **A** to **Z**. Start at the ★.
Color the picture.

© Rainbow Bridge Publishing

Match the letters in the code to the numbers. Use the code to answer the question.

What is the name of a young cat?

___ ___ ___ ___ ___ ___
17   15   26   26   11   20

Connect the dots from **1** to **29**. Count by 2s.
Start at the ★. Color the picture.

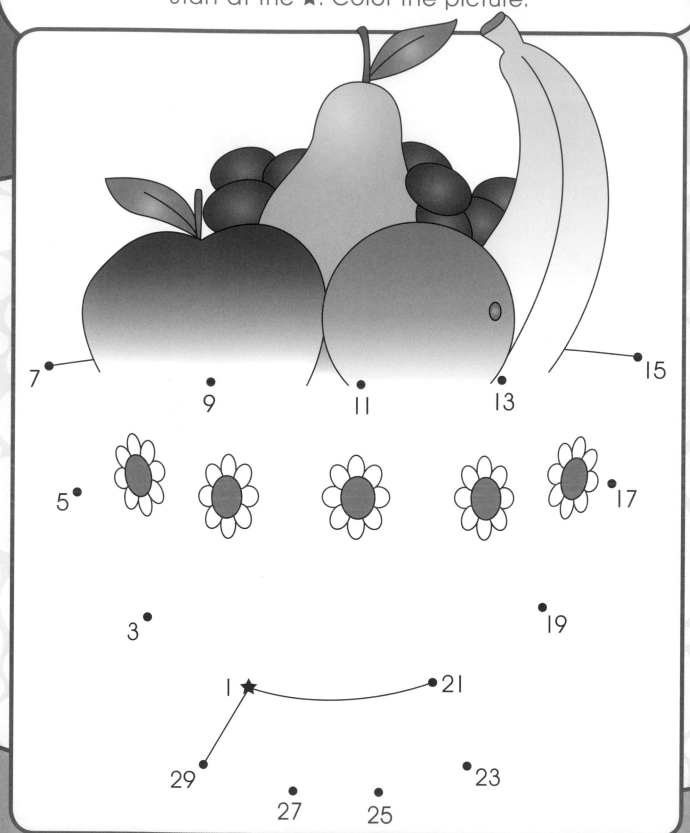

© Rainbow Bridge Publishing

Cut out the puzzle pieces. Put the puzzle together.

Match the letters in the code to the numbers. Use the code to answer the question.

What is the name of a band of colors
you see in the sky after it rains?

___ ___ ___ ___ ___ ___ ___
24   7   15   20   8   21   3

Connect the dots from **1** to **29**. Count by 2s.
Start at the ★. Color the picture.

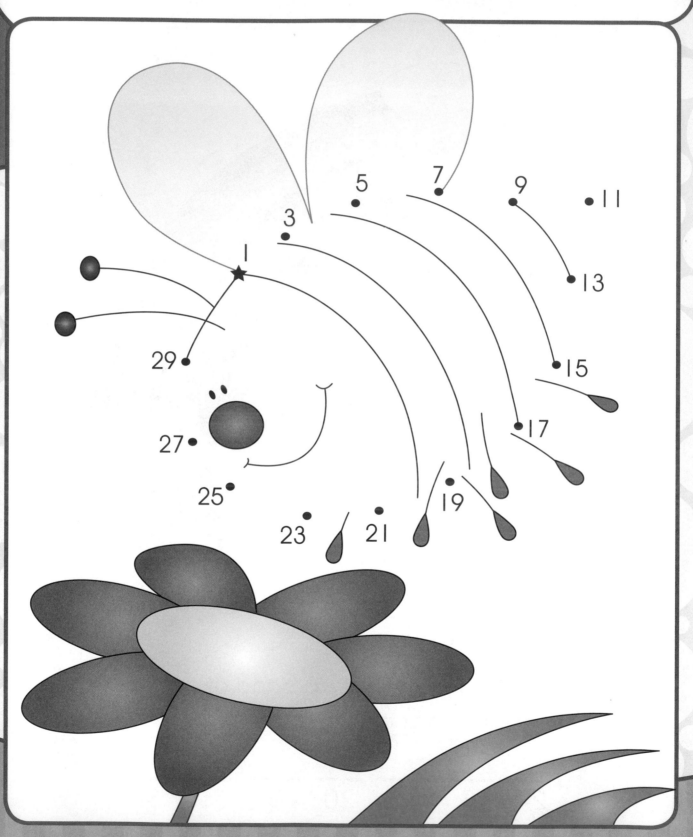

© Rainbow Bridge Publishing

Connect the dots from **A** to **Z**. Start at the ★.
Color the picture.

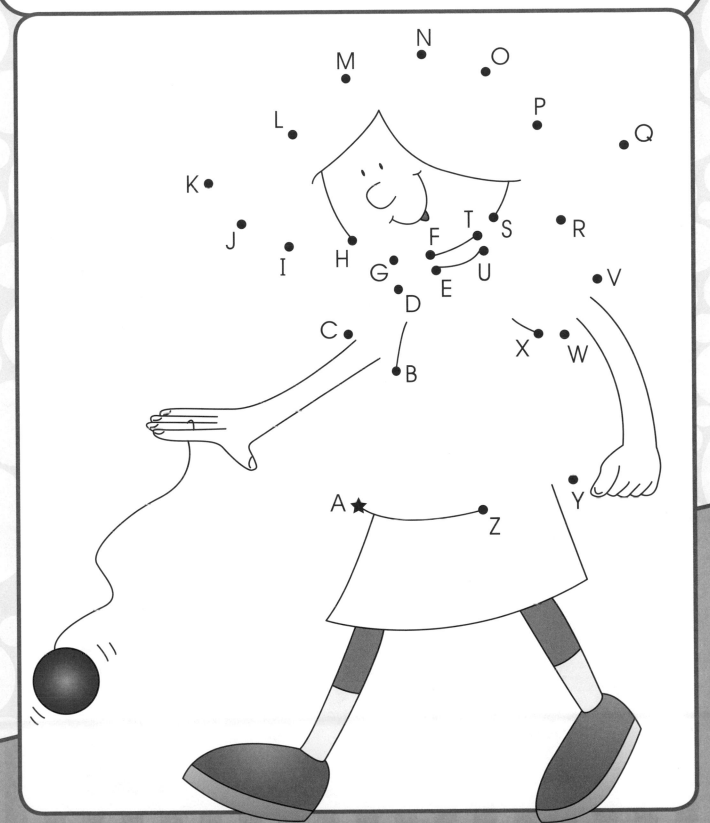

© Rainbow Bridge Publishing

Connect the dots from **5** to **50**. Count by 5s.
Start at the ★. Color the picture.

© Rainbow Bridge Publishing

Cut along the dotted lines. Fold along the solid lines to make the flowerpots stand up.

cut

© Rainbow Bridge Publishing

Break the code and find the letters to
name a type of big cat.

5	K	I	E	C	Z
4	N	O	K	J	R
3	P	I	N	B	U
2	C	N	G	Y	M
I	A	W	O	N	M
	A	B	C	D	E

| | | | | | |

5D 4B 3E 2C IA 4E

© Rainbow Bridge Publishing

Connect the dots from **A** to **Z**. Start at the ★.
Color the picture.

© Rainbow Bridge Publishing

Connect the dots from **A** to **Z**. Start at the ★.
Color the picture.

Break the code and find the letters to name a type of tree.

5	H	N	B	J	M
4	T	A	S	U	D
3	C	X	K	P	Q
2	V	L	W	I	F
I	O	G	E	Y	R
	A	B	C	D	E

5E 4B 3D 2B 1C

© Rainbow Bridge Publishing

Cut out the puzzle pieces. Put the puzzle together.

cut

© Rainbow Bridge Publishing

Connect the dots from **10** to **100**. Count by 10s.
Start at the ★. Color the picture.

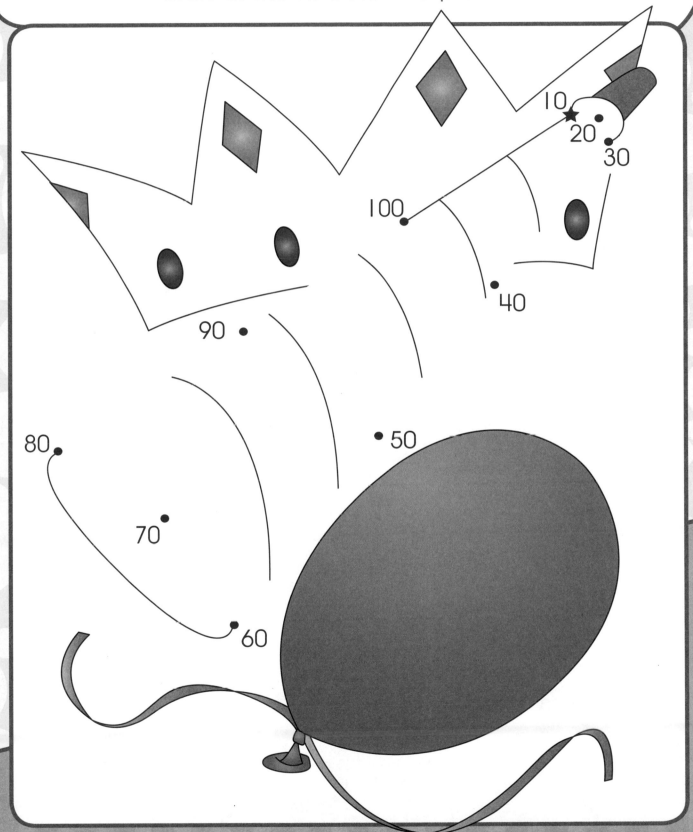

10
20
30
100
40
90
80
70
50
60

© Rainbow Bridge Publishing

Use a different color crayon to trace each pipe.

Which pipe has the leak?

© Rainbow Bridge Publishing

Cut out the puzzle pieces. Put the puzzle together.

cut

Match the letters in the code to the numbers.
Use the code to answer the question.

5	P	R	F	O	B
4	J	W	C	P	K
3	V	A	Q	X	H
2	D	S	I	L	T
1	N	E	U	M	G
	A	B	C	D	E

Eating what fruit each day
keeps the doctor away?

3B 4D 5A 2D 1B

© Rainbow Bridge Publishing